Bernd Schlösser

Lithops

Flowering Stones

A Practical Guide For The Successful Windowsill Grower

About the Author

The author was born in Berlin - Spandau, Germany, in 1960. Although pursuing a profession in banking, he has, since early childhood, been devoted to the animal and floral kingdoms, where insects and succulent plants attracted his particular attention.

His initial interest in cacti was soon replaced by a novel object of affections coming dramatically into focus when, at age 14, he happened to notice his first Lithops plant - a Lithops lesliei - in the window of a f lower shop.

Impatiently and completely at a loss to know what kind of plant it was, he had to wait for the shop to open, which was, however, so much the worse since all this happened on a weekend, and Monday morning was still far away.

Because of its shape, this strange naked gnome reminded him of a mushroom, yet nothing of what little knowledge the youngster had about plants would conveniently fit the picture.

When sunlight got trapped inside them, the dark-green little windows on top of the plant, which was about four cm high, began to shine mysteriously; whereas the skin all around the sides appeared like velvet.

This love at very first sight deepened very quickly to become a passion and, till today, it has not waned.

Contents

Preface

The objective of this booklet . . .

Comprehensive and reliable literature on the genus Lithops is, indeed, still scarce. The few books dealing extensively with this subject (see the chapter on "Recommended Literature and Specialised Commercial Sources") are either out of print or available only with greatest difficulty. Furthermore, the prices paid by avid collectors often far exceed $/£ 100.00.

In some of the many books on house-plants, cacti, and other succulents, there is one page, or even less, dedicated to Lithops, and not always are the cultivation hints given for them quite correct. For example, they recommend temperatures of 15°C/59°F for resting the plants in winter, but we shall see later on why such temperatures must be avoided under all circumstances.

Fortunately, the continuously growing interest in the genus Lithops is accounted for by a steady increase in supply from specialised commercial sources making more and more - and even rare and difficult - species available to the plant enthusiast.

Despite all this, when interviewed by the author about 'Flowering Stones' (in German more often referred to as 'Living Stones'), most of the people did not understand the meaning of this term, nor did they know much, if anything at all, about the proper treatment and cultivation of these plants.

In the long run, the plant lover can enjoy a plant only if he is fully familiar with its proper care and if he bothers to master and apply the few - but essential - skills and tricks of the trade. The work as presented here has the objective to pass on a many years' experience in a comprehensible and clear arrangement. May it help the reader to become more successful and self-assured in his practical work with these oddities of the plant world. In turn, this would greatly enhance the appeal and popularity of the genus.

Last but not least, it is appropriate to mention here that the devoted grower of such plants contributes in an invaluable manner to nature conservation through the preservation of species. The natural conditions in which the Flowering Stones prevail in habitat have already been and, on an ever increasing scale, continue to be damaged or totally destroyed by Man who massively undermines functional ecosystems, e.g. with farming operations, expansion of infrastructures, and growing tourism.

Bernd Schlösser

Lithops lesliei ssp. lesliei var. minor C006

Cultivation Notes - a Briefing in 'First Aid'

For more detailed information, refer to the appropriate chapters.

Plant Situation
- in summer: move plants to a place with very bright to full sunlight
  (protection against blazing noontime sun is vitally important),
  in warm position with adequate movement of air (but no draft!)
- in winter: plenty of light and low temperature (6–10° C).

Watering
Less is more; do not water turgid plants, but modest waterings can be given if the plant bodies begin to show wrinkles. Do not water at all during the resting period (ca. December to April).

When the plants are kept cool already in November, ensure that the soil has dried completely.

Soil
must be well-draining; one part grit (or coarse sand) and one part sifted peat with some loam.

Feeding
during the vegetation period (May - October) at intervals of 3 to 4 weeks.

Lithops julii ssp. julii C349

Morphology and Natural Environment of the Genus Lithops

The genus Lithops belongs into the plant family of Mesembryanthemaceae (midday flowers) - well known by the short term 'Mesembs' to the amateurs of these succulents. So far it comprises 40 species, not taking into account the additional number of respective subspecies and varieties.

The name 'Lithops' (derived from Greek 'lithos' = stone and 'opsis' = appearance) itself hints at the amazing resemblance between the plants and the stones surrounding them; it is this particular phenomenon which allows them to employ one of their most obvious survival strategies. The otherwise defenceless plants have developed forms and features adapting them to their physical environment with such perfection that it is extremely difficult to spot them in habitat. Even the rediscovery of plants that have just been spotted on the ground may become a strenuous task if the beholder's attention is turned elsewhere for a moment.

This ingenious ruse - adaptation of their outward appearance to the immediate inanimate surroundings or physical environment is described as 'crypsis', whereas the terms 'mimicry' and 'mimesis' are often used incorrectly because they apply to instances where visible characters adapt to, or imitate, the animated environment (e.g. animals and plants). Making a virtue of necessity, plants in cultivation fortunately retain their beautiful coloration and pattern of camouflage.

When speaking of "Flowering Stones" in a stricter sense, we actually refer to Lithops plants even though there are still other genera whose morphological features serve the same strategy, e.g. Argyroderma, Conophytum, Dinteranthus, Lapidaria, Ophthalmophyllum (regarded to be a section of Conophytum by Steven Hammer), Pleiospilos, Tanquana (separated from Pleiospilos in 1986), Titanopsis, and others more.

A great deal of them have another feature in common, i.e. fenestration or translucent windows, at the thickened upper leaf ends or leaf tips (typically occurring in the genera of Fenestraria, Frithia, and Haworthia).

Because, in their natural habitat, the plants are usually buried "up to the neck" in soil, their opportunities are rather limited to "brandish" their foliage towards the sun for photosynthesis to take place. Instead, they have developed a sophisticated strategem to catch light without having to give up their hiding places. The light striking the plant window is deflected by the various patterns of markings which are intrinsic to each species and genus. The water-storage tissue inside the succulent leaf then disperses the light in such a manner that it is reflected onto the chlorophyl-holding sidewalls where it is utilised for photosynthesis.

Lithops are nothing more than a pair of leaves almost completely fused together as evolutionary adaptation to the extreme scarcity of water in their natural environment took its course. These highly succulent leaf-pairs - efficient in storing water or organic moisture - function as a reserve of sustenance against periods of drought; and dry spells are indeed a frequent occurrence in their arid environment.

Another key feature of morphology in these plants is their compact dwarf growth form. Their miniaturism, on the one hand, enables the plants to mitigate the environmental condition of draught by colonising in the shade of stones, under small trees and tufts of grass, and in the cracks of rocks. On the other hand, their compact growth form (approximating a globular shape) allows for a maximum capacity to retain vital fluids linked with a minimum of superficial evaporation deficits. The general outline of a Lithops plant is turbiniform inasmuch its shape resembles a top or an inverted cone.

Lithops occur naturally in the Republic of South Africa (mainly in the Transvaal and Orange Free State) and in Namibia as well. Often they may be found - if one is indeed lucky enough to spot them - on the shaded side of low quartz-gravel slopes or gentle inclines. The sites where they grow embedded between cracks in rock formations, as noted above, are well protected, and during their resting period they are often completely covered by sand. The plants occur in colonies comprising a small number of specimens on a few square metres, or populations of up to several hundreds on a larger territory.

In such habitats, the markings on their leaves (lobes) - often reticulated and veined - blend in with the rocks and stones among which they live (sandstone, quartzite of all forms and colours, jaspis, feldspar, gneiss, granite, etc.). Taxonomically, such markings provide the main criteria to distinguish between the ranks of species, subspecies, and variety within the genus.

Distinctive characteristics to be mentioned here include the shapes and colorations of islands, peninsulas, size of windows, dashes, lines, and channels between the windows, as well as various types of translucent or dark-brown dots in the epidermis.

The top surface may also be grooved, smooth, rugose, and flat and/ or convex, respectively. The structure of the gaping or narrow fissure (shape, depth, length) and the profile of the lobes (rounded, elliptic, reniform, or cordate) are accorded additional significance. A few botanists who carried out profound studies on the genus have designed so-called analytical keys for the identification and recognition of species, generally based on the principle of presence or absence of criteria (exclusion keys). If it is, in fact, reasonable to use them at all, these keys can be helpful to classify and recognise a species only in the ballpark since it is impossible to describe in exact words e.g. localised forms with all their minor, and even minutest, variations. Such keys are apt to get you on the wrong track rather than on the home straight, failures being pre-programmed.

After repeated unsuccessful attempts at working with a key, the author has now come to adopt D.T. Cole's position that it is probably impossible to produce an efficient key for the genus Lithops. Certainly, with the acquisition of an extensive working experience from practical study of a multitude of plants, one would be on a great deal firmer ground.

The individual plant bodies are quite variable in size, and there may be considerable differences, sometimes even within a single species. Large Lithops species (e.g. L. aucampiae, L. pseudotruncatella) attain sizes of 50x35 mm (length x width measured across the fissure) or more. The smallest species (L. dinteri ssp. frederici) has an average size of ca. 14x10 mm.

At the beginning of the vegetation period, a new little body starts emerging from deep inside the plant where it develops on the growing point (meristem) at the tip of the stem over the rootstock. It increases in size at a considerable rate of speed and soon pushes upward through the continuously widening cleft.

The fluid contained in the old little body is completely absorbed by the new leaf-pair until, finally, there remains nothing but the papyrus-like sheath of the old body, now enveloping and protecting the plant. After the old leaves have been replaced, the new leaf-pair should be all that makes up a healthy plant. It is possible that the new growth splits, thus allowing two new little bodies to emerge, tightly nestled at first, but only to end up in gradual separation and final divorce.

The new bodies consist of decussate leaf-pairs, which means they are arranged at roughly right angles relative to the old leaf-pairs. In habitat, the replacement of leaves occurs also during periods of drought, whereas flowers usually develop only when there is sufficient moisture available to the plant.

Referring to the life span of cultivated plants, experienced collectors have reported that at an advanced age (from ca. 10 years up) the plants are prone to get fussy about their care and to react more squeamishly to possible mistakes. Lithops in habitat can survive for many decades and reach a remarkable age. An age of almost 100 years has been reported, but this case might provide an exception to the general rule.

Sometimes, however, exceptionally severe periods of drought do take a heavy toll amongst Lithops since even these masters of survival can not persist without receiving a drink once in a while.

The author himself became a witness to the generosity of some farmers in Namibia who, just for this reason, would occasionally treat the Lithops on their land to a thoughtful sip of the noble liquid. More than a little was he pleased one day to be given the opportunity to carry out this honourable task himself.

To answer the question as to how the genus Lithops should be most successfully cultivated and attended to, we need to first consider the pivotal importance of the following: conscientious study and gaining knowledge of the particular circumstances of survival in the natural environment (habitat).

Taking this as a starting point for all further reflections about cultivation is as deceptively simple as it is helpful; being applicable to all forms of life on this planet Earth - be they vegetable, animal, or human - it is a law of nature, so to speak. This cognisance of "rearing close to nature" shall be made available and put into practice in the following chapters.

Now we have a look at some habitat-pictures:

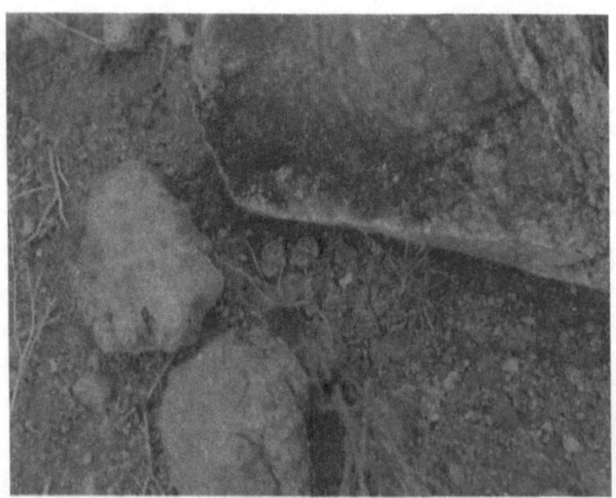

Lithops karasmontana ssp. bella C285

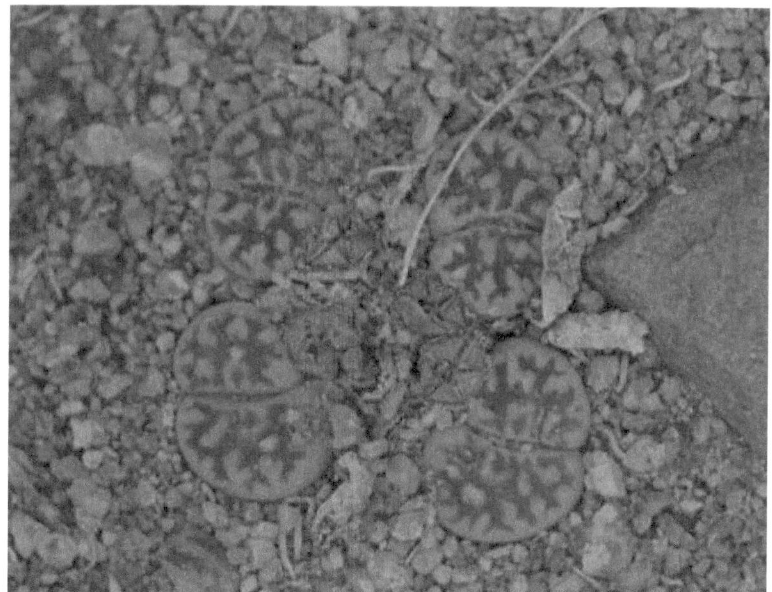

Lithops karasmontana ssp. bella C285

Photo showing site of the above illustrated specimens. The small town of Aus, Namibia, can be seen in the left background.

You have to give all of your attention......

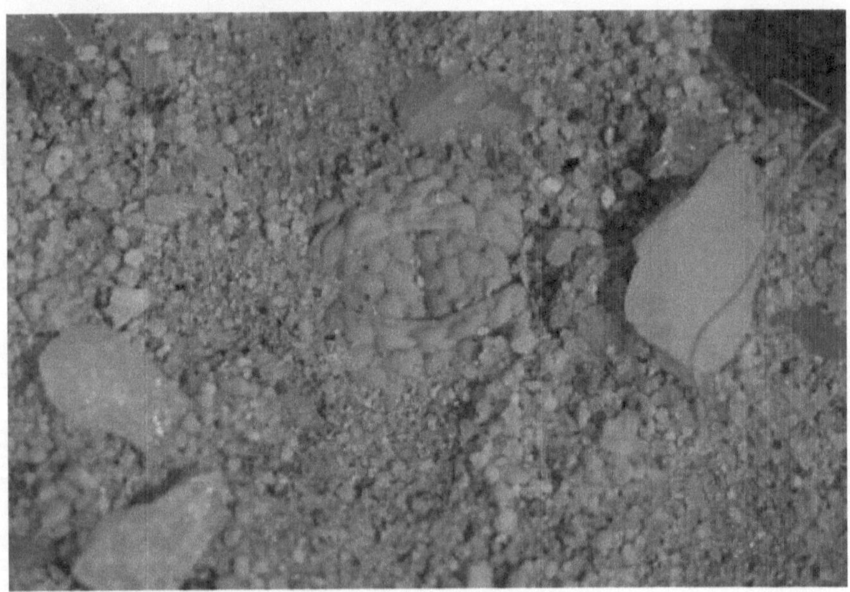

Lithops gracilidelineata ssp. + var. gracilidelineata
(on the farm „Wüstenquell")

Lithops gracilidelineata ssp. + var. gracilidelineata
(on the farm „Wüstenquell")

Lithops schwantesii ssp. + var. schwantesii
(on the farm „Sinclair")

Lithops schwantesii ssp. + var. schwantesii
(on the farm „Sinclair")

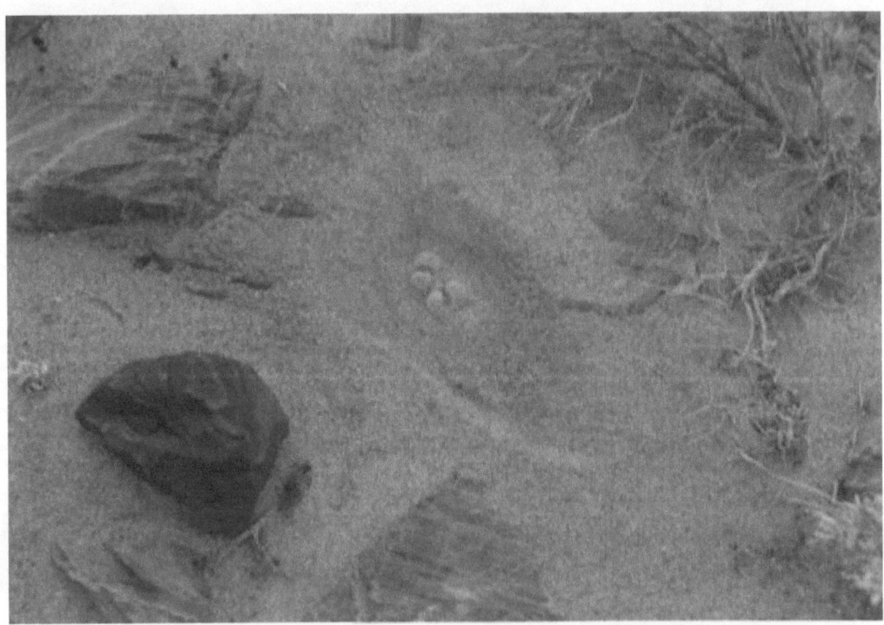

Lithops optica in the „Sperrgebiet" near Pomona, Namibia

Major Distribution Areas

drawing A

The Parts of the Plant-Body

drawing B

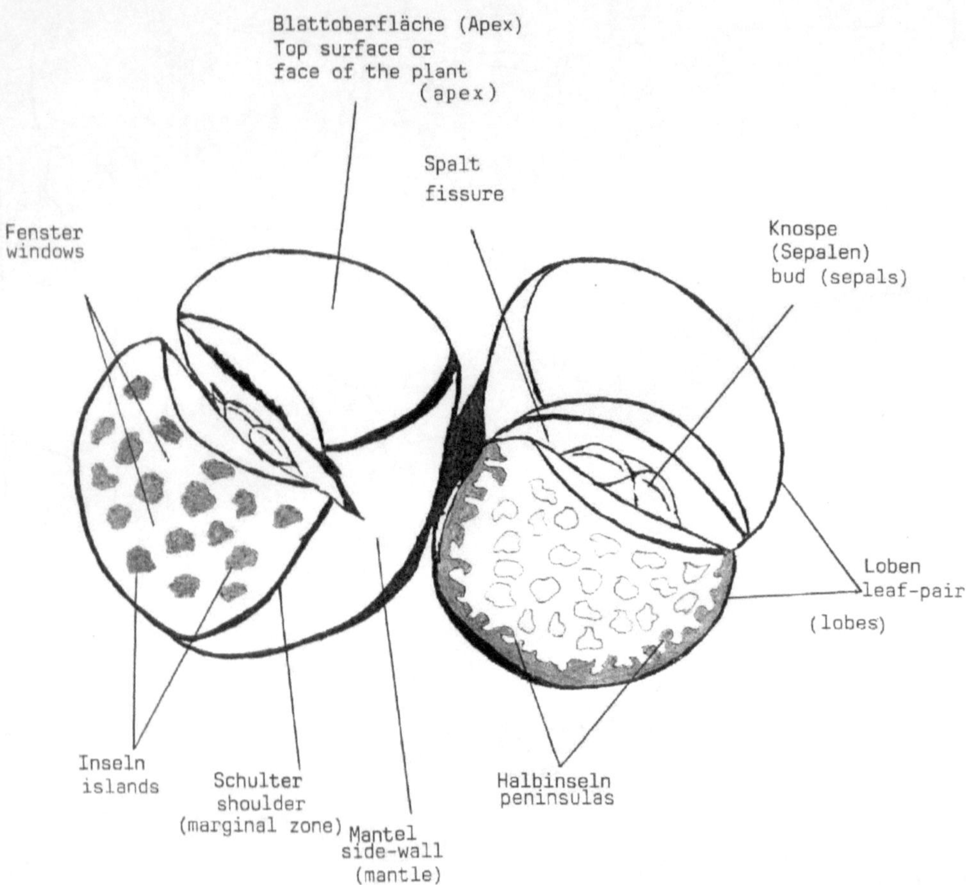

Soils and Fertilisers

The composition of soils at the habitats varies from one location to the other, depending on the different types of rock formations occurring there, and these, in general, are not very rich in nutrients. We cultivate all species of the genus in a <u>freely draining</u> substrate consisting of one part gravel (or coarse sand) well mixed with one part sifted peat and some additional loam. Commercial mixes for sowing and transplanting are very suitable when used as aggregates.

In any case, too much humus, peat, compost, or similar soils should be avoided because they are compositions derived from rotting plant substances, which are likely to harbour, or favour growth of, fungi or bacteria, resulting in an eventual infestation of the plant. Under normal circumstances these organisms are not present in the wild, or they occur but sparsely, which explains why Lithops have developed almost no resistance against them.

Reference to the soil mix used for sowing will be found under the appropriate heading 'Propagation from Seed' (page 36).

Individual soil mixtures are not less numerous than the individuals dedicated to Lithops. Therefore, the above information, which is based on general experience, should be understood as a recommendation. There are no limitations imposed on anyone who wants to carry out his own experiments!

Although Lithops have adjusted to a frugal diet, in cultivation they should rather be treated to regular feedings (every 3 to 4 weeks) using a commercial well-balanced potplant or cactus fertiliser during the vegetation period (e.g. 8+8+6, which means containing 8% nitrogen, 8% phosphorus, and 6% potassium). Make sure to observe the instructions for recommended dosages!

Seedlings also - or especially - should be given fertilisers on a regular basis because it helps them notably in developing the plant bodies. A lack of nutrients in Lithops (e.g. caused by exhausted or deficient substrates) can be recognised by the following symptoms, which may occur simultaneously on the same plant:

· The plant exhibits a distinct paleness; particularly the beautiful colorations on the top of the lobes seem to be vague and watery

· the plant has a translucent, vitreous appearance

· the epidermis looks conspicuously thin and is more vulnerable to environmental influences (agents promoting decay can attack more easily and eventually destroy the plant)

· the plant fissure undergoes a transformation causing it to resemble a pair of closed tongs or a clasping claw.

· shortly after having completed its annual replacement of leaf-pairs, the plant produces another body which is characterised by its elongated and vigourless appearance, while losing the healthy turbiniform shape resembling an inverted cone.

In the majority of cases, the ailing plant will not recover easily. An attempt at saving it by cautious repotting and regular feedings (water carefully!) may turn out successful; however, it will take some time to replace the old leaves before the unsightly condition is corrected.

Lithops karasmontana ssp. + var. karasmontana (mickbergensis „summitatum") C168

Transplanting

In order to avoid any unnecessary stress to the plants, adult specimens should not be repotted more often than every three to four years, unless the substrate has become too limy due to the use of hard water. Transplanting Lithops into a fresh substrate while they are budding will cause them to react most likely with the premature withering and loss of flowers. When repotted, Lithops can also be particularly sensitive to waterings because any possible lesions to the plant body and root system must be first allowed to heal. Therefore is it necessary to keep the plant completely dry for about 7 to 10 days, while direct sunlight must be avoided. The stress of repotting may cause our fosterling to put on a somewhat wrinkly face but none the worse for that since the genus is used to water shortages.

Repotting of the plants can be done at any time - and is especially called for when they are under attack from disease or pests. The best time, however, is between June and August because the growth of the new leaves, on the one hand, is completed by then and most specimens, on the other hand, have not yet started to flower. Besides that, Lithops regenerate better and faster during the period of active growth than during the murky months of winter.

As experience shows, the plant recovers quickly after its curative rest, as soon as watering is resumed, with the skin (epidermis) becoming taut: This is a good indication that our little darling has started to root again. Warm feet will help considerably in promoting the rooting process; heating mats serving that purpose can be obtained from specialised retailers (see page 66).

Lithops plants bought from commercial sources are sometimes planted in nothing but humic composts or peat; they should be repotted as soon as possible.

In general, there are no objections against embedding cultivated Lithops as deeply in the soil as they occur naturally in the wild: the windowed top surface almost level with the surrounding ground (see photos of specimens in habitat). Admittedly, this form of cultivation does bear its risks, and some experience with the genus is indispensable since the sensitive stem area above the roots (meristematic region), being buried at a deeper level, does not dry off quickly and thus may serve as a gateway to rot. Therefore, the less experienced Lithops enthusiast is well advised to promote his protégé(e) to a more exposed or elevated position.

An addendum to transplanting seedlings (page 39): having reached an adequate size after about 6 months, the plantlets should be thinned out, spacing them approx. one inch (2-3 cm) apart. It is recommended to prepare a pot with fresh substrate and to dig little holes in the soil with the tip of a pencil or a similar instrument. Then the delicate roots can be accommodated carefully in the cavity by using the blunt end of the pencil to push up some soil against them and to refill from the sides of the hole.

When choosing the most suitable containers for transplanting, one should keep in mind that Lithops, and particularly the older specimens, can develop tap-roots of a remarkable length. Consequently the pots or trays should be at least 8-10 cm high. A tip: square plastic pots help save a lot of space.

Lithops gracilidelineata ssp. gracilidelineata var. waldroniae acf Fritz` White Lady C189A

Light, Ventilation and Temperature

The regions of South Africa and SWA/Namibia are the natural home of Lithops, which explains that this genus needs plenty of light to develop compact vigorous bodies and to prevent etiolation. A window or, preferably, a balcony facing south is ideal to account for the plants' great appreciation of plenty of fresh air, and to facilitate the night-time gas exchange which supports their metabolism.

Due to the fact that most arid regions are characterised by severe cold during the early morning hours, our Lithops have permission to spend their night-time on the balcony during the summer months; but not so when there are extended periods of cool weather accompanied by rain.

When taking a closer look at the sites where the plants grow naturally in habitat, it is interesting to note how they are protected from the blazing midday sun. Frequently they can be found on the shaded side of a small hill or slope, in crevices, behind rocks of small or larger size, and sheltered by tufts of grass, or shrubs. Consequently, it is essential that plants in cultivation, too, receive some protection during hot afternoon hours to prevent wasting away their strength.

This holds true particularly for seedlings in their first year when they are prone to get burnt quickly by the intense sunlight in summer; in this case a sunny window facing west would be more suitable.

What our fosterlings have in common with human beings is the need to adjust gradually to the increasing amounts of sunlight when the winter months are over, lest they suffer sunburn. Good ventilation is another important factor to protect the plants from damage.

Watering

In their natural environment, Lithops, for many months in the year, depend entirely on morning dews and fog to satisfy their need for moisture.

Being true masters of the art of survival, Lithops should be watered according to the motto 'Less is more'! This might ensue in watering too scarcely, but an overdose can be administered a good deal faster, with fatal results to the plant. A plant body fed too generously is apt to burst. Pathogens can then enter the ugly cracks - occasionally deep tears - and cause the spreading of rot, which is almost impossible to control.

As a general rule, it is recommended to rather saturate the soil once thoroughly than to distribute the same amount of water in small portions over a number of days. Waterings should be resumed only after the substrate has dried out to a considerable extent. There should be extra provisions for good water drainage because Lithops hate being kept 'with their feet wet' all the time.

It is preferable to use decalcified water (every department store sells suitable and easily applied water softeners for little money) or it should at least be left standing for a while.

The following schedule may be helpful for your watering regime:

<u>April:</u> Misting with distilled water

<u>May :</u>   Begin watering **carefully** as new growth becomes visible and old leaf-pairs have been almost completely absorbed by the new little bodies.

<u>June - October :</u> A good cue and rule of thumb for watering is a distinct shrivelling on the sides of the plant bodies. Wrinkles appear especially pronounced on hot summer days as a result of the plants' exposure to direct sunlight in the afternoon (see previous chapter). Mistings, given in the evening hours, with distilled water or clean rain water are

gratefully accepted (not so, however, when flowers are still open). Waterings, too, are more appreciated in the evening for the following two reasons:

<u>Firstly:</u> The plants recover better during the cooler hours at night and benefit for a longer time from the moisture of the substrate (frequently the wrinkles disappear before next morning).

<u>Secondly:</u> Drops being splashed on the plants while watering can have the effect of a small lens and cause ugly burn marks. This is easily avoided in the evening when the intensity of sunlight is greatly diminished. The plant amateur should make it a principle to carefully remove any such drops left from watering with a paper napkin.

Especially in September Lithops respond extremely well to watering. After a splashing one can almost watch them growing.

<u>November:</u> Waterings should now cease; the soil must dry out completely to prepare for the resting period. (If at this time, e.g. some plants are still actively engaged in flowering and one might wish to continue watering, care must be taken to raise the temperature accordingly!).

With regard to watering, the months of <u>December to March</u> direct our attention to the following discussion of cultivation in winter.

Lithops villetii ssp. deboeri

Cultivation in Winter ('Hibernation')

The resting period of Lithops occurs during our winter (in the northern hemisphere) which means that in their native environment the plants go dormant during the summer season of the southern hemisphere. During this period, Lithops cease all active growth - at least when judging from what is superficially visible - (whereas the tiny new body is being 'delivered' at this time).

It is essential to take this behaviour into consideration because cultivation will not induce the plants to reverse their natural growth pattern. Even the specimens grown from seed under our conditions do not deviate from these biologically determined facts.

In autumn, one should stop watering early enough so that the moisture still present in the soil may dissipate before the hibernation period begins. **Cold and persistently wet conditions are obnoxious to all Lithops species and will cause the death of the plants.** Moisture of condensation from a high atmospheric humidity must be avoided for the same reasons.

It follows that no waterings should be given in winter even if plants shrivel up a little. This is less the case at temperatures ranging from 6° C to a maximum of 10° C (43-50° F) because the genus then inactivates its metabolic system, and the plant body stops evaporating moisture.

Normally the plants are not tolerant of frost, although several of the more robust species can withstand temperatures below the level of 0° C/32° F (down to approx. -6° C/21° F) for a short period of time (some hours). Complete dryness of the soil is, however, an essential precondition.

At home, Lithops may occasionally be exposed to mild frost in the morning hours. One must keep in mind, however, that the soil in which the plants are embedded in habitat still retains some of the previous day's heat, thus compensating considerably for the degrees of cold at ground level.

In winter, the plants should be so accommodated that - just as in summer -they receive an optimum of light (with no draft); they do quite well in a sunny basement window or in a small conservatory. Using heated rooms as winter quarters would be completely inadequate for Lithops plants.

In May, as Lithops start revealing their revamped bodies, waterings may be resumed, but starting with care and scantiness. The spring cleaning campaign (starting in April) can include light mistings with distilled water to remove the dust accumulated in the winter months from the old plant bodies and to spur growth of the new ones.

The cultivation hints given above are applicable to countries in the northern hemisphere where, generally, cold winters prevail. Cultivation in regions with mild or warm winters - primarily in the southern hemisphere - allows for a more generous watering regime. After a sunny day, this permits light mistings in the evening, whatever the season may be. Such practice simulates the dews and fogs occurring in habitat at night and in the morning hours. Besides that, one can start watering carefully as early as the end of March/beginning of April.

Lithops karasmontana ssp. karasmontana var. lericheana
Lithops ruschiorum „nelii“ (below)

Proper care is usually sufficient to prevent these unpleasant conditions or to reduce at least the possibility for infections to spread in the first place.

The key symptom hinting at some sort of ailment in a plant is its flaccid or sickly appearance.

One should make it a rule to inspect the roots of **any** plant immediately after its acquisition. Undesirable stowaways ready to invade the collection can thus be literally stifled at birth.

Here then is it appropriate to list the most common pests and diseases from which our pet plants may suffer.

Mealy-Bugs and Root Lice

As indicated by the name, these pests are rootstock dwellers. They are white in colour, ca. 1 mm in size, and their shape suggests a similarity with pill bugs. Not infrequently, they also invade terrain above ground level where they hide in clefts and cracks on the plant body. With some dexterity, however, is it possible to pick off these superficial parasites.

In order to get rid of the little "mealies" that cling to the delicate root system, it is necessary to pot out the plant and to examine its rootstock very carefully and cautiously. The cotton-like nests produced by the animals are easy to spot and must be removed completely.

Mealy-bugs and root lice tap the roots of the plants and withdraw nutrition over a length of time.

Soft Rot (Wet Rot)

This is the worst enemy of the genus and has almost the same significance for Lithops as a civilizational disease because plants living in the wild are rarely confronted with an over-abundance of water and compost-loving fungi, typically the principal agents of disease.

Once a plant is infected, there remains little hope to save it. Not more than a few hours are necessary for the soft rot to permeate the entire plant and to cause it to collapse like a mass of jelly. Its putrid odour is what makes it unpleasantly conspicuous.

To keep the infestation from spreading, it is best to separate the plants. Infected bodies on multiheaded specimens must be removed immediately with a sharp knife. If possible, everything should be disinfected afterwards, and the - repotted - plant must go into quarantine for several weeks.

Damping - Off

Batches of seedlings are the target of such an unfriendly take-over which causes their tender bodies to become glassy and to collapse within a minimum of time. One can try to salvage whatever can be salvaged by using a weak solution of Chinosol (from the pharmacy or drugstore). As a precaution against the fungus which induces damping-off, the soil should be thoroughly disinfected before sowing. For more details refer to "Propagation from Seed".

Epidermal Disfigurations

Plants have occasionally been observed to produce patches of odd, and ugly, corky skin or dry, irregular blemishes. It is known of thrips - 2-4 mm long insects - that they can cause this kind of damage. However, after carrying out a painstaking surveillance of the plants, the author was unable to discover any of these little beasties, even though they can be easily spotted with the naked eye. The cause of this damage has remained an unsolved problem to the author, but it is suspected that fungal spores or bacteria could have entered the fissure of the old plant and attacked the very delicate skin of the newly forming body. This hypothesis is supported by the fact that, in the majority of cases, it was always a single little head on a polycephalous (multiheaded) plant to become affected in this manner. So it seems unlikely that a disease - presumably starting from the roots - could have spread out to infect the entire plant. It is interesting to note that, frequently, the plants in question had been flowering the previous year. Such minor disfigurements are merely superficial and the problem is rather a cosmetic one. Mostly, these "defects" will melt away with the regeneration of growth in the coming vegetation cycles.

Plants cultivated outdoors can sometimes fall prey to birds' beaks which can be recognised from triangular bite marks in the epidermis. Admittedly, these marks are unattractive, but hardly threatening to the plant's health provided the laceration is kept as dry as possible until scar tissue has formed (dusting with charcoal powder disinfects, and boosts the healing process). By next spring, with renewal of the leaf-pair, the little mishap telltale will be gone anyway.
In this context it should be mentioned that not every bug crawling over our plants necessarily bears a stress potential for us. Parasitic wasps have been observed building their nests in plant trays without doing harm to any of the little plants.

As much as possible, all diseases and pests should be controlled without using a chemical bludgeon, but in some instances it becomes unavoidable. Most garden centres and nurseries are able to supply the suitable remedies. (In Germany it is mandatory for the distributor to provide adequate information before selling the product).

Natural Predators

The regions where Lithops occur naturally are, of course, also inhabited by many enemies who eat them, such as:

>   Birds (guinea-fowl, bustards, ostriches),
>   Rodents (hares, ground squirrels, rats, mice),
>   Larger Mammals (springbok, goats, sheep),
>   Insects (grasshoppers, beetles, crickets, bugs and mites, worms,
>   grub etc.),
>   Other animals (tortoises).

This list does not claim to be complete.

It is noteworthy that Lithops are more prone to become victims of predators during periods of particularly severe drought.

This only serves to demonstrate the reasons why good camouflage is so essential for Lithops. The unarmed little bodies have, indeed, no other choice but to hide, and particularly so since they cannot even produce poison.

It has been reported that native nomads, roaming the vast regions of Africa, have occasionally appeased their thirst by eating the plants.

With regard to conservation of the genus, all this could, perhaps, still be a tolerable situation, but far more to blame for the increasing destruction of this natural wonder is Man himself.

Fortunately, the majority of South African succulents are protected under nature conservation programs, but what is the use of even the most reasonable laws when hardly anyone abides to them; or when they are poorly enforced; or when simply abolished, by reason of state, for the benefit of construction projects.

Abnormalities

From time to time, mother Nature likes to test something new on her children, and not even Lithops plants can trust on being spared.

This bears reference to spontaneous and permanent changes in the genetic material (mutations), which constitute a fundamental factor in the evolutionary process. Once the transformed species has gained the ability to prevail within its given environment (process of natural selection), it is also successful in passing on its genes to the next generation.

a) Colour Aberrations

- Plant body:

These changes can be seen very distinctly within the genus when comparing the, sometimes, very conspicuous colour-aberrations (green, green-yellow, red) of the plant body with the type species.

After all, it is a vital question of survival for these plants to match their colour patterns as perfectly as possible to their close environment. Thus one may indeed wonder why adult specimens were found in habitat manifesting rather conspicuous colorations. This implies that - despite their striking appearance - they were deceiving their enemies for a remarkably long time.

Occasionally it happens that mutations which were previously unknown in cultivation are discovered among batches of seedlings. Such most attractive novelties of Nature have been received with an interested welcome from collectors. They are systematically propagated and distributed by special succulent nurseries and may be recognised - if their labelling is correct - by the cultivar status indicated with the plant name (discussed under "Future Perspectives", page 68).

The survival chance of these flashy Lithops is, of course, a great deal better in the protected atmosphere of cultivation.

- Flower colour:

Flower colour represents another variant within the genus that is determined by genetic mutations.

There are some forms that produce white flowers although these should, normally, be yellow; but no instances are known of typically white-flowering species to produce yellow flowers instead.

It should be annotated that the dimensions of the plants (shape, configuration) are not affected by aberrations in the body or flower colours; aberrant variants are just as vigorous and reproductive as are the true type species.

b) Deformities

Occasionally, one comes across plants with fissures that divide them into more than the usual two lobes.
Most of these cases involve trilobed specimens, but even four-lobed and multilobed plants have been observed. Sometimes even the tiny bodies of cotyledons already manifest three lobes.

In seedlings up to the third or fourth year, the phenomenon of three lobes is not a rare occurrence. This whim of Nature may appear incidentally in mature plants, only to disappear again the following year when the new little body is formed.

Owing to their ephemeral appearance, multiple lobes and similar deformations of the fissure are not to be regarded as mutations in the proper sense.

Plants manifesting such phenomena neither benefit nor suffer from them; normally they are healthy, vigorous, capable of reproduction, and by no means inferior (a say-so not entirely new to the author).

A very rare exception to the rule is the cristata-form. Such plants never showing a flower and can not produce seed. The form of the lobes does not disappear and the plant keeps it for the whole life.

Selecting Plants for a Personal Collection

Due to the dwarf growth form of Lithops is it possible to accommodate a considerable number of plants although the available space may be rather limited. They are not turned off by living in crowded conditions or even skin to skin. Lithops seem to enjoy buddying up, and one cannot avoid the impression that sociably they thrive better.

When buying Lithops, you should take care not to acquire any beefed-up exemplars. With a little bit of practice, you can recognise them by their unnaturally big size and bloatedness. In most cases, the enthusiast will not cherish them for a long time since such plants, having been raised speedily under greenhouse conditions with overdoses of nutrients and ample water, were never given a chance for hardening. When subsequently treated under normal conditions, they become often prone to diseases (particularly soft rot) or attacks from pests. Otherwise, but in the best possible case and with diligent pampering during the next vegetation cycles, they can regain their natural size by going on a "recuperative shrinkage cure".

As a kick-off, the following list with robust and more sensitive species may help the novice to select his/her plants. The robust species will more readily tolerate a minor blunder in cultivation (which must not become a habit though), as for example overwatering.

<u>Very robust:</u> Lithops aucampiae, L. hookeri (formerly turbiniformis), L. karasmontana ssp. karasmontana var. lericheana L. olivacea

<u>Robust:</u> Lithops bromfieldii, L. coleorum, L. hallii, L. lesliei, L. pseudotruncatella, L. salicola, L. schwantesii, L. terricolor (formerly localis)

<u>Normal:</u> Lithops divergens, L. dorotheae, L. fulviceps, L. gesineae, L. helmutii, L. karasmontana (remaining species), L. optica, L. steineckeana (here, some fellow collectors may be in disagreement; see the discussion on "The Myth of Lithops steineckeana"), L. verruculosa, L. werneri

<u>Sensitive</u>: Lithops dinteri, L. francisci, L. gracilidelineata (plants readily take up lots of water and puff up to enormous size, just to die from soft rot; keep them starving!), L. julii incl. fulleri "clan", L. marmorata, L. otzeniana, L. ruschiorum, L. villetii

<u>Difficult</u>: Lithops comptonii, L. meyeri cv. 'Hammeruby', L. vallis-mariae, L. viridis

<u>Special guidelines for the cultivation of Lithops optica (incl. acf 'Rubra')</u>: This species is not quite easy; in comparison to all the other Lithops species it has a growth cycle which is "shifted" backwards by two to three months, i.e.:

	shifted:	normal:
dormancy starts in	January/February	December
vegetation starts in	June/July	April/May
flowering period	December	Sept./October partially also November

(All information approximated)

Even in its resting period, Lithops optica never seems to "fall asleep" completely. The plants start shrivelling slightly after a few weeks despite the fact that temperatures may have dropped to 8 or 10° C. This signifies that the plant body is evaporating moisture and making use of its metabolism (through assimilation). The flowering time occurs in our winter (in the northern hemisphere) when the months are gloomy, while the plant refuses to adjust its growth cycle accordingly. This makes it almost impossible for us to ever see a flower without resorting to technical aids, in this case artificial lighting.

It is recommended to use the following strategy for the cultivation of this species:

During dormancy, maintain slightly higher temperatures than required for the rest of species (12-15° C) which permits light mistings at regular intervals. This practice can be adopted without any qualms because the natural habitat of the species is located in immediate vicinity to the coast in Namibia ("Sperrgebiet" south of Lüderitz). Thus, it receives moisture almost daily from fog banks and dew, while temperatures drop, occasionally, to severe cold in the morning hours. Apart from that, all of the familiar rules for cultivation still apply to this case.

Lithops julii ssp. fulleri var. fulleri

The Myth of Lithops steineckeana

An interesting story has been woven around this species.

It made its first appearance in the Steinecke Nursery at Ludwigsburg, near Stuttgart, where it emerged in a batch of Lithops seedlings. Presumably, the seeds had gotten among other seed of this genus. As there were no records, the origin of the seeds could not be traced back with certainty. Other seedlings of the same age, however, had been grown from seed coming from Great Namaqualand (SWA), and thus it was assumed that the species originated from there.

Other assumptions suggest that Lithops steineckeana is in fact a hybrid. Based on certain conclusions and criteria, there is reason to believe that Lithops ruschiorum (for its shape and general features) and Lithops pseudotruncatella (for its coloration, markings, and flower structure) are the possible "parents".

More evidence in support of this assumption is provided by additional criteria that all three of the species have in common, that is, they share the same - and peculiarly early - flowering time (late July-August) as well as the proximity of their habitats.

Regarding the species "steineckeana", a locality where it occurs naturally in the wild has not yet been discovered.

Several botanists (Dr. Hendrik W. de Boer, B. Fearn, and Ernst B. Fritz) who had studied the genus for many years had since tried to obtain seed of Lithops steineckeana from interbreeding the putative parents; all these experiments proved unsuccessful.

More recent hybridisation projects involving additional Lithops species and even representatives of other genera were carried out by Steven Hammer (1999), but also failed to produce the desired results. Further tests with Conophytum calculus are under consideration. Hammer does not exclude the possibility that both parents of L. steineckeana were of hybrid origin themselves.

According to the literature, one may experience difficulty in sowing or growing this species because the, initially successful, germination of the seed (precise details are lacking, unfortunately) is followed by the death of most of the seedlings within two or three months.

In contrast to all this, B. Fritz (1981) observes that not only was germination excellent, but the seedlings also grew vigorously, with just a few losses. Specimens planted out on his rockery would survive more successfully than even the local L. lesliei.

The author's own experiments met with extremely poor germination results.

At the end of February 1997, 64 grains of seed of this species were sown; germination of 4 seeds occurred after 7 and 10 days. Two of them turned out to be very feeble weaklings and died within a few days. The remaining two seedlings showed good growth and, after increasing considerably in size in 1998 and 1999, now make a robust and promising impression.

Lithops steineckeana C388

Propagation from Seed (Sexual reproduction)

Sowing Lithops offers a good opportunity to acquire numerous plants whose availability from commercial sources might otherwise be a matter of pure chance, or sheer impossibility. Information on how to obtain seeds can be found under the heading "Recommended Literature and Specialised Commercial Sources" (see page 65).

More often than not, seed packets sold in garden centres and nurseries bear information such as: "Mostly flowers in the first year". Such statements, though not absolutely false, boast of a truly exceptional achievement because, normally, it takes Lithops at least three years to flower, with the provision of adequate growing conditions, as e.g. in the greenhouse. Expectations are grossly exaggerated in this case.

The seeds are preferably planted in early March. So, the little plants can make progress with the gradual approach of summer and increasingly better light conditions.

The growing medium is composed of equal parts of coarse sand (gravel) and sifted topsoil. The golden rule in sowing is to ensure the best possible sterility in order to protect the very tender seedlings against all kinds of diseases.

Therefore, it is strongly recommended to steam the sand and the sifted topsoil separately before sowing. The steaming can be done in a cooking pot of sufficient size, and the process should be extended over at least several minutes to kill the germs, while care must be taken not to burn the topsoil.

After cooling down, both components are then mixed together. The containers for sowing, and for storing the water used in sowing, should also be sterilised; this can be accomplished by using a plant sprayer to spray these utensils with a weak Chinosol solution. During the first 6-8 weeks, the water supply should be decalcified and boiled for later use.

The soil mix (of which we retain a small portion) is then slightly soaked with the prepared water and filled into the pots or trays. Next, the fine seeds are sprinkled over the substrate and, after sifting the saved soil mix lightly over them, are soaked carefully by applying a fine misting from the sprayer which has been cleaned of the Chinosol. The seed containers now need to be kept in a well-lighted - not sunny - place, at temperatures between 15 - 20° C (59-68° F).

For the next 6-8 weeks the substrate must be constantly kept damp, but not wet, preferably by watering from the bottom; it is essential not to allow the pots to dry out.

A most appreciable solution when propagating from seed, is the use of a mini propagation box, which can be obtained from garden centres for a few dollars/pounds. The high air humidity is beneficial for fast germination, and the little plants make good progress. Care should be taken to provide sufficient movement of air in warm weather conditions - especially on a sunny day - because the seedlings can be burnt quite easily (utmost caution is advisable against an over-exposure to bright sun)!

Seedlings can take a lot more moisture than adult plants. When the seedlings have reached a good size, after 2-3 months, it is but a venial sin if, occasionally, the substrate is allowed to dry out superficially.

During the germination phase - for ca. 4 weeks - the sowing pots should not be moved, and drafts should be avoided. Good circulation of air is beneficial (do not cover the sowing containers with plastic foil, etc.).
The first cotyledons may be expected to appear after 5-7 days of germination. It is noteworthy that the plants to break out first from the protective seed coat are the ones appearing to be the most vigorous and robust.

All this may seem like an elaborate mumbo jumbo for sowing, but the devout plant lover will be rewarded with many healthy and strong seedlings going far to express their gratitude in their own sweet way.
The germination rate is always somewhat higher than the plants' later survival rate, which is an entirely normal situation. It is estimated that in the natural environment of the genus there is, on the average, only one single plant to survive out of 1000 seeds originally dispersed, and to reach final maturity. So it makes sense that the small seed capsules contain a very large number of seeds, a few hundred in most cases. In cultivation, we yield much better results. There have been some reports of germination rates close to 100 % (under greenhouse conditions), whereas results of 40–50% attained on the windowsill may be regarded as excellent.

Lithops fulviceps var. fulviceps acf Aurea C363
(seedlings approx 4 weeks old)

Lithops fulviceps var. fulviceps acf Aurea C363
(seedlings approx. 6 months old)

The first resting period in winter is the first opportunity for the seedlings to really prove their valour because they tend to dry up if they did not have a chance to "rat themselves fat". It is astounding to see how nonchalantly seedlings of pinhead size can manage to make their way through such harsh periods of want, while others - ca. half a centimetre big - struggle in agony, only to be saved by the first splash of water coming with the next vegetation period.

Despite reasonable sowing conditions, it may happen that some species fail to germinate. There is a possibility that the seed was too fresh as one should allow the seed 1-2 years of storage after harvesting. An overaging of the seed can be excluded almost with certainty because Lithops seed will often remain viable even for 15-20 years. This is one of Nature's ingenious designs because, in the wild, rainfall events are scarce commodities; and it may happen that, over many years, moisture availability remains insufficient for an assured survival of the young sprout.

If germination still has not occurred after several weeks, you can let the sowing pot dry off and put it on stand-by, so to speak, until next year when you may try your luck again.

Another interesting and clever mechanism comes into play every time our batch of seedlings are watered again, by continually triggering a new wave of seedlings over a period of several weeks. In the natural environment of the genus, this kind of safety mechanism has a purpose. It keeps the seeds from germinating all at once on the very first rainfall event, and prevents the possibility of total wipe-out during subsequent draughts. Thus, at least a portion of seeds, by "sitting out" dry periods, can take advantage of the next down-pour, and of the one after it, for drawing their first breath.

Once the seedlings have gained enough strength, you should begin, as soon as possible, with their gradual and cautious adaptation to sunlight and treat them like adult plants; this will make them sufficiently strong and hardy. The little Lithops plants can be planted out after approx. 6 months when most of them have already recycled their first leaf-pairs. For subsequent cultivation it is advisable to select only the most vigorous seedlings because, in the majority of cases, weaklings will stay retarded also in the future.

Next to growing plants from acquired seed, it is another enjoyable and economical endeavour to raise them from seed harvested by yourself. In order to ensure that the produced offspring is of true breed, a desirable objective among collectors and propagators, it is absolutely necessary to pollinate two flowering specimens of exactly the same species, subspecies, variety, etc. This is most conveniently done with the help of a small, soft brush. Gently move it with alternating strokes over anthers and stigmas to exchange the pollen. If the succulentophile wishes to obtain true-bred offspring, screening with fine gauze should be employed as a precaution against any transfer of foreign pollen via insects, to exclude possible hybridisation.

Regularly, Lithops flowers are white or yellow, or, in some cases, orange in colour. Under normal conditions it is impossible to successfully cross-pollinate flowers with different colours. If seed sets at all, it will be deficient and not yield viable seedlings, or at best rather sickly ones; certain species, however, provide for the rare exception to this rule.

It is assumed that the white and yellow flowering species now subsumed under the genus Lithops have developed independently from each other (parallel evolution). Nature's ingenuity devised the same thing twice, as one might put it, but each time the flower colours were different. This process whereby plants adopt a great similarity with regard to their shape, appearance, and survival strategy is termed evolutionary convergence (morphological adaptation). Genetically, however, there are obvious differences that become clearly manifest in the course of successive breeding procedures.

It is, of course, possible to pollinate different Lithops species having the same flower colour with each other. The seeds thus obtained can indeed produce attractive bastards (hybrids), but their use for further breeding is doubtful since the genetic material will probably segregate in the succeeding generations (F1, F2…) with the result that the progeny will no longer resemble their parents (cf. the Mendelian principles of heredity).

The genus' flowering season falls into the months of September to November. The flat, seemingly compressed buds always emerge solitary pushing their way upward through the fissure, while growing towards light. The protective leaves or calyx segments called sepals, - usually numbering five - are also succulent and bear tiny, pellucid dots.

Self-pollination of the flowers being improbable, if not impossible to occur (self-sterility, self-incompatibility), it usually needs a second plant to tango and set seed successfully (here, too, the exception proves the rule). An equally fruitless effort would be to try and outwit multiheaded specimens with several flowers. Also see the discussion in the section on ”Propagation from Cuttings“.

Lithops flowers vary in size - as do the little bodies. They open in the afternoon and stay open until close to sunset, not infrequently covering the whole plant body. The more often the flowers open and close (for 5-7 days), the more they increase in size. This is triggered by growth of the cells in the petals which controls the opening and closing mechanism.

When pollination has been successful, a fruit with mostly 5–7 segments or partitions (loculi) starts developing under the withered flower.

After the mature capsule has become dry about 6-8 months later, it is ready for another stunning performance. Water perchance dripping on the hygroscopic seed capsule activates a swelling mechanism (hygrochastic function) which opens the partitions that enclose the seeds. In habitat, these are splashed out as more drops of rain fall down on them.

Having dried off after the rainfall event, the seed capsule closes up again. The remaining seeds are thus preserved, and, safely packed, wait for the next shower of rain to come.

In cultivation, the best method for the amateur when harvesting the seeds, which vary in size from one species to the other, is to carefully crush the diligently collected capsules between the fingers and to separate the debris from the seed.

Pollination of Lithops in habitat is achieved with insects, such as bees, wasps, butterflies, flies, beetles, etc., acting as pollinators.

seed capsule, closed

seed capsule, open

Propagation from Cuttings (Vegetative reproduction)

Sooner or later, Lithops plants tend to divide and become multi-headed. The degree of consistency of this phenomenon varies with individual species, so that there are some developing only a few heads (e.g. L. aucampiae, L. gracilidelineata, L. pseudotruncatella) and others forming substantial clusters e.g. L. bromfieldii, L. olivacea, L. optica, L. ruschiorum). But this is just another instance in which to expect deviations from the rule, and a species, generally notorious for its reluctance to divide, can become truly addicted to polycephaly, in an isolated case.

Under normal conditions, Lithops karasmontana ssp. karasmontana var. lericheana will hardly produce more than 3-5 heads, but there are records of a specimen (ca. 10 years old) which, in 1999, had already built a 'hemisphere' of 30 heads and continues to multiply every year. It is suspected that this excessive polycephaly may be caused by some genetic deficiency. However, this seems not to be associated with any disadvantage to the plant since it thrives and flowers abundantly.

In the spring of 1998, the same plant produced a small head with a double fissure, similar to the one illustrated on page 82 in D.T. Cole's book (Fig. 23). This in turn gave birth to three healthy and normal-shaped bodies in the following year. Concededly, the occurrence of a double fissure in the genus Lithops is extremely rare, but not absolutely unique.

Apparently it makes sense for the plants to divide because it can be conceived as helpful for their survival. If one of the small bodies is, perchance, destroyed by a predator, it will not at all impair the plant's ability to stay alive. Some species are, perhaps, less endangered by natural enemies, and this could be the reason for them not to divide so readily, at the cost of excluding this vital conservation aspect from their survival strategy.

Collectors can capitalise on polycephalous tendencies because it is possible to obtain a number of individual plants within a short time, which can then be used e.g. as trade-offs for other sought-after specimens. With rare species, this can also serve as an excellent strategic move to stay in good supply. Should a plant become affected with disease and die, substitutes are immediately available and your discomfort stays within reasonable limit (note that soft rot can also infect adjacent heads on the same plant).

Lithops enthusiasts should, however, keep in mind that the genus is self-incompatible and, for a pollination to be successful, usually requires a second plant which cannot be a cutting originally taken from the first plant.

Now let's turn practical: carefully remove the plant you want to cut apart from the pot. Using a very sharp knife (better even, a razor blade), cut off the chosen little head in such a manner that a small stub of the rootstock remains on the cutting (it's essential!). Make sure to avoid lesions to the water-storage tissue because they can induce rot. The cutting is placed in a dry substrate (see discussion on "Soils and Fertilisers") and must not be watered for ca. 7-10 days, while the same applies to the repotted parent plant.

Finally, it seems appropriate here to discuss the phenomenon of "adventitious sprouting" (propagules): In contrast to the above explained division, which takes place inside the plant body due to the regeneration of growth, adventitious sprouts occur ("externally") on the body. In this process, a new little body develops on the meristem of the plant without, however, being protected by the layer of old leaves.

Such adventitious sprouts are extremely rare; only two of them have been observed by the author in the course of 20 years. Astonishingly, they occurred on two very young seedlings of L. dinteri ssp. multipunctata (approx. one year old) and L. optica acf Rubra (approx. 9 months old). But these seedlings were feeble, and their prognosis contradictive to longevity. (Addendum: L. optica acf Rubra seems to have a tendency to adventitious sprouts. This have been observed in a few cases.)

A Short Excursion into Nomenclature

The scope of this subject - for most of us a rather tedious and complicated one - is not meant to touch on more than the most important aspects. Those are, in fact, the ones we might have to cope with on a daily basis once we start studying plants more thoroughly.

In this field, as in many spheres of our life, we are at the mercy of red tape and bureaucrats with their unrestrained mania to regularise and establish rules of operation.

The International Code of Botanical Nomenclature (ICBN) and a similar work for the identification of cultivated plants (ICNCP) was conceived and adopted by scientists collaborating world wide. In the course of many years, the first-mentioned catalogue of rules has swelled to almost 80 Articles and paragraphs. It is constantly being revised, extended, and amended on the botanical congress which meets every six years. It prescribes that a plant, or rather its name, is only then validly published and recognised when all pertinent rules have been meticulously adhered to.

It is easy, even for a graduated botanist, to become entangled in its highly complicated and stiff rules and, considering all this, the well-disposed reader shall be spared such tedious lecture.

Taxonomy is a classification system of biological categories following a hierarchical order. In a hierarchy of ranks, the criteria for differentiation of single individuals become more and more subtle and extended the farther one proceeds from the broadest to the narrowest level.

The following example gives the full designation of a plant:

Lithops dinteri ssp. dinteri var. dinteri acf Dintergreen (1985)

Lithops = genus
dinteri = species
ssp. = subspecies

var. = varity

acf. = aberrant colour form (formerly cv. for cultivar = cultivated variety

Often, the epithet is followed by the curtailed form of the author's name and the year of its publication. Even two names can, sometimes, be mentioned, one of them in parentheses. In such a case the plant was possibly given a new rank, or it was even transferred into another genus, as a consequence of new evidence and research, whereas the old name now appears in parentheses followed by that of the new taxonomist.

For the sake of clarity, the study as presented here can well do without such names, considering their irrelevance for our daily routine, while using them is correct practice as far as nomenclature is concerned.

All botanical names of Lithops taxa have a specific origin and are published in latinized form. Some are named for the discoverer or informant as well as for the collector or his wife; or the epithet describes certain features of the plant, such as shape, coloration, markings in the leaf tips, etc., etc.

It is a pity that commercially available plants are often labelled simply "Flowering Stone", thus causing occasional difficulty for even the experienced Lithops lover in assigning the correct name to a particular specimen.

Lithops vallis-mariae; the rough surface of the lobes, a characteristic feature of this species, can be easily recognised.

Locality Data Lists

This list was originated by Desmond T. Cole (reference). It enumerates all the various species, subspecies, varieties, etc. together with the respective locality data pertaining to their individual areas of distribution.

Here, it offers us a good opportunity to present an overview of all the names designating the various Lithops species. It enables us to become familiar, and to compare them, with the labels we may encounter. Some amendments will surely become necessary in course of time, and it does not claim completeness (C = "Cole Collection Number").

Each of the following epithets are preceded by the generic name "Lithops":

Cole Fieldnumberlist Lithops (numerical order)

C001   lesliei ssp. lesliei var. venteri/30 km nw Warrenton, SA (= South-Africa)
C002   aucampiae ssp. aucampiae var. aucampiae/near Danielskuil, SA
C003   aucampiae ssp. aucampiae var. aucampiae/10km se Postmasburg, SA
C004   aucampiae ssp. aucampiae var. aucampiae/5 km n Postmasburg, SA
C005   lesliei ssp. lesliei var. lesliei (Warrenton form), SA
C005A   lesliei ssp. lesliei var. lesliei acf Albiflora/near Warrenton, SA
C006   lesliei ssp. lesliei var. minor/25 km sw Swartruggens, SA
C006A   lesliei ssp. lesliei var. minor acf Witblom/25 km sw Swartruggens, SA
C007   lesliei ssp. lesliei var. lesliei/15 km s Johannesburg, SA
C008   lesliei ssp. lesliei var. lesliei (grey form)/70 km w Mafikeng, SA
C009   lesliei ssp. lesliei var. lesliei (grey form)/70 km w Mafikeng, SA
C010   lesliei ssp. lesliei var. lesliei/25 km sw Lobatse, B (= Botswana)
C011   aucampiae ssp. aucampiae var. aucampiae (Kuruman form)/5 km sw Kuruman, SA
C012   aucampiae ssp. aucampiae var. aucampiae (Kuruman form)/10 km e Kuruman, SA
C013   hookeri var. dabneri/25 km s Kimberley, SA
C014   lesliei ssp. lesliei var. lesliei (Kimberley form)/15 km nw Kimberley, SA
C015   lesliei ssp. lesliei var. hornii/40 km sw Kimberley, SA
C016   aucampiae ssp. aucampiae var. koelemanii/35 km nw Postmasburg, SA
C017   lesliei ssp. lesliei var. rubrobrunnea/5 km nw Randfontein, SA
C018   lesliei ssp. lesliei var. lesliei/near Stella, SA
C019   hookeri var. subfenestrata (brunneoviolacea)/40 km sw Griquatown/Griekwastad, SA
C020   lesliei ssp. lesliei var. lesliei (luteoviridis)/15 km w Magaliesburg, SA
C021   hookeri var. subfenestrata/15 km ssw Prieska, SA
C022   hallii var. hallii/55 km sw Prieska, SA
C023   hookeri var. hookeri (vermiculate form)/55 km sw Prieska, SA
C024   julii ssp. fulleri var. fulleri/5 km n Kenhardt, SA
C025   verruculosa var. glabra/30 km e Kenhardt, SA
C026   lesliei ssp. lesliei var. lesliei/60 km sw Johannesburg, SA
C027   lesliei ssp. lesliei var. lesliei/near Bethlehem, SA
C028   lesliei ssp. lesliei var. lesliei/10 km n Harrismith, SA
C029   lesliei ssp. lesliei var. lesliei/45 km ne Vaalswater, SA
C030   lesliei ssp. lesliei var. lesliei (Pietersburg form)/30 km nw Pietersburg, SA

C031   lesliei ssp. lesliei var. lesliei/10 km ne Meyerton, SA
C032   lesliei ssp. lesliei var. lesliei (Pietersburg form)/10 km se Pietersburg, SA
C033   lesliei ssp. lesliei var. lesliei/45 km e Pietersburg, SA
C034   salicola/10 km nw Luckhoff, SA
C035   hookeri var. marginata/25 km se Hopetown, SA
C036   lesliei ssp. lesliei var. lesliei (Warrenton form), SA
C036A   lesliei ssp. lesliei var. lesliei acf Albinica/near Warrenton, SA
C036B   lesliei ssp. lesliei var. lesliei acf Storms´s Albinigold/near Warrenton, SA
C037   salicola/40 km se Hopetown, SA
C038   hookeri var. lutea/5 km ne Groblershoop, SA
C039   hallii var. ochracea/5 km ne Groblershoop, SA
C040   bromfieldii var. bromfieldii/15 km ene Upington, SA
C041   bromfieldii var. bromfieldii/15 km ene Upington, SA
C042   bromfieldii var. insularis/15 km e Keimoes, SA
C043   bromfieldii var. insularis/15 km e Keimoes, SA
C044   bromfieldii var. mennellii/25 km ssw Upington, SA
C045   hallii var. hallii/15 km sw Upington, SA
C046   aucampiae ssp. aucampiae var. aucampiae/5 km ne Griquatown/Griekwastad, SA
C047   lesliei ssp. lesliei var. venteri/30 km w Warrenton, SA
C048   aucampiae ssp. euniceae var. euniceae/15 km n Hopetown, SA
C049   salicola/10 km nw Petrusville, SA
C050   hallii var. hallii/15 km se Strydenburg, SA
C051   hookeri var. hookeri (vermiculate form)/15 km nw Strydenburg, SA
C052   hallii var. hallii/25 km sse Hopetown, SA
C053   hookeri var. marginata (red-brown form)/25 km sw Douglas, SA
C054   aucampiae ssp. euniceae var. fluminalis/near Hopetown, SA
C055   olivacea var. olivacea/25 km sw Pofadder, SA
C056   julii ssp. fulleri var. fulleri/25 km sw Pofadder, SA
C056A   julii ssp. fulleri var. fulleri acf Fullergreen/25 km sw Pofadder, SA
C057   bromfieldii var. insularis/10 km ne Keimoes, SA
C058   marmorata var. marmorata (framesii)/45 km ene Springbok SA
C059   hallii var. ochracea/10 km nw Upington, SA
C060   vallis-mariae/30 km ssw Mariental, Namibia
C061   aucampiae ssp. aucampiae var. aucampiae/70 km wsw Vryburg, SA
C062   julii ssp. fulleri var. fulleri/near Kakamas, SA
C063   julii ssp. julii/60 km se Warmbad, Namibia
C064   julii ssp. julii/near Karasburg, Namibia
C065   karasmontana ssp. + var. karasmontana (Signalberg form)/25 km wnw Grünau, Namibia
C066   vallis-mariae/20 km e Gibeon Station, Namibia
C067   pseudotruncatella ssp. + var. pseudotruncatella/20 km ene Windhoek, Namibia
C068   pseudotruncatella ssp. + var. pseudotruncatella (alpina)/35 km sse Windhoek, Namibia
C069   pseudotruncatella ssp. volkii/45 km s Windhoek, Namibia
C070   pseudotruncatella ssp. + var. pseudotruncatella/30 km s Windhoek, Namibia
C071   pseudotruncatella ssp. dendritica (pulmonuncula)/50 km wnw Rehoboth, Namibia
C072   pseudotruncatella ssp. dendritica/65 km wsw Rehoboth, Namibia
C073   pseudotruncatella ssp. dendritica/95 km wsw Rehoboth, Namibia
C074   schwantesii ssp. schwantesii var. urikosensis (christinae)/50 km w Maltahöhe, Namibia
C075   schwantesii ssp. schwantesii var. urikosensis (nutupsdriftensis)/35 km w Maltahöhe, Namibia
C076   schwantesii ssp. schwantesii var. schwantesii/70 km w Maltahöhe, Namibia
C077   schwantesii ssp. schwantesii var. schwantesii/near Helmeringhausen, Namibia
C078   gesinae var. annae/25 km sw Helmeringhausen, Namibia
C079   schwantesii ssp. schwantesii var. schwantesii/25 km sw Helmeringhausen, Namibia
C080   schwantesii ssp. schwantesii var. schwantesii/30 km sw Helmeringhausen, Namibia
C081   optica/10 km w Lüderitz, Namibia
C081A   optica acf Rubra/10 km w Lüderitz, Namibia
C082   karasmontana ssp. eberlanzii/35 km e Lüderitz, Namibia

C083   schwantesii ssp. schwantesii var. urikosensis/near Bethanien, Namibia
C084   dinteri ssp. dinteri var. brevis/20 km se Vioolsdrif, SA
C085   hookeri var. dabneri/35 km w Kimberley, SA
C086   salicola (maculate form)/35 km se Hopetown, SA
C087   hallii var. hallii (salicola reticulata)/30 km se Hopetown, SA
C088   hookeri var. marginata (cerise form)/20 km ene Hopetown, SA
C089   hookeri var. marginata (red-brown form)/25 km nw Hopetown, SA
C090   hallii var. hallii/50 km nw Hopetown, SA
C091   hookeri var. susannae/30 km se Douglas, SA
C092   hookeri var. elephina/10 km n Britstown, SA
C093   hookeri var. elephina/25 km ne Britstown, SA
C094   hallii var. hallii/45 km se Prieska, SA
C095   verruculosa var. verruculosa (inae)/55 km sw Prieska, SA
C096   lesliei ssp. lesliei var. lesliei (Warrenton form)/25 km n Kimberley, SA
C097   pseudotruncatella ssp. pseudotrunc. var. riehmerae (edithiae)/50 km se Windhoek/Namibia
C098   hallii var. ochracea/50 km nnw Upington, SA
C099   pseudotruncatella ssp. + var. pseudotruncatella (mundtii)/150 km ne Windhoek, Namibia
C100   pseudotruncatella ssp. + var. pseudotruncatella (mundtii)/135 km ne Windhoek, Namibia
C101   ruschiorum var. ruschiorum/35 km ne Swakopmund, Namibia
C102   ruschiorum var. ruschiorum (nelii)/20 km e Cape Cross/Kaap Kruis/Namibia
C103   ruschiorum var. ruschiorum/45 km ene Henties Bay, Namibia
C104   pseudotruncatella ssp. archerae/120 km nw Maltahöhe, Namibia
C105   schwantesii ssp. schwantesii var. urikosensis/100 km nw Maltahöhe, Namibia
C106   schwantesii ssp. schwantesii var. schwantesii/80 km w Maltahöhe, Namibia
C107   schwantesii ssp. schwantesii var. urikosensis (christinae)/20 km w Maltahöhe, Namibia
C108   karasmontana ssp. bella/5 km s Aus, Namibia
C109   olivacea var. olivacea/10 km n Pofadder, SA
C110   hookeri var. hookeri/50 km nw Marydale, SA
C111   hallii var. ochracea/35 km wnw Prieska, SA
C111A   hallii var. ochracea acf Green Soapstone/35 km wnw Prieska, SA
C112   hookeri var. hookeri/40 km wnw Prieska, SA
C113   hookeri var. hookeri/10 km nw Niekerkshoop, SA
C114   hookeri var. hookeri/15 km nw Niekerkshoop, SA
C115   lesliei ssp. lesliei var. lesliei/5 km nw Vryburg, SA
C116   bromfieldii var. glaudinae/70 km wnw Griquatown/Griekwastad, SA
C117   aucampiae ssp. aucampiae var. aucampiae/45 km nw Griquatown/Griekwastad, SA
C118   hookeri var. hookeri/25 km w Strydenburg, SA
C119   hallii var. hallii (grey form)/30 km wsw Strydenburg, SA
C120   verruculosa var. verruculosa/30 km n Vanwyksvlei, SA
C121   julii ssp. fulleri var. fulleri/115 km w Kenhardt, SA
C122   julii ssp. fulleri var. fulleri/125 km w Kenhardt, SA
C123   villetii ssp. kennedyi/90 km sse Pofadder, SA
C124   dorotheae/15 km n Pofadder, SA
C125   comptonii var. comptonii/50 km ene Ceres, SA
C126   comptonii var. weberi/70 km s Calvinia, SA
C127   viridis/25 km s Loeriesfontein, SA
C128   otzeniana/35 km nnw Loeriesfontein, SA
C128A   otzeniana acf Aquamarine/35km nnw Loeriesfontein, SA
C129   verruculosa var. verruculosa/30 km e Brandvlei, SA
C130   terricolor/30 km sw Rietbron, SA
C131   terricolor (peersii)/near Miller Station, SA
C132   terricolor/40 km e Laingsburg, SA
C132A   terricolor acf Silver Spurs/40 km e Laingsburg, SA
C133   terricolor/25 km s Beaufort West, SA
C134   terricolor (Prince Albert form)/5 km n Prince Albert, SA
C135   hallii var. hallii (brown form)/20 km se Strydenburg, SA

C136   hallii var. hallii (brown form)/35 km ene Strydenburg, SA
C137   hookeri var. marginata/35 km e Hopetown, SA
C138   lesliei ssp. lesliei var. lesliei/near Benoni, SA
C139   lesliei ssp. lesliei var. lesliei/5 km e Benoni, SA
C140   francisci/35 km e Lüderitz, Namibia
C141   lesliei ssp. lesliei var. mariae/10 km sw Boshoff, SA
C142A   hallii var. ochracea/30 km nw Niekerkshoop, SA
C142B   hookeri var. hookeri/30 km nw Niekerkshoop, SA
C143A   karasmontana ssp. bella/60 km nne Aus, Namibia
C143B   schwantesii ssp. schwantesii var. schwantesii/60 km nne Aus, Namibia
C144   schwantesii ssp. schwantesii var schwantesii (grey form)/55 km nne Aus, Namibia
C145   schwantesii ssp. schwantesii var. schwantesii/55 km ne Aus, Namibia
C146   schwantesii ssp. schwantesii var. schwantesii/55 km ne Aus, Namibia
C147   karasmontana ssp. eberlanzii (erniana)/40 km s Aus, Namibia
C148   schwantesii ssp. schwantesii var. marthae/60 km sse Aus, Namibia
C149   karasmontana ssp. eberlanzii (erniana witputzensis)/110 km sse Aus, Namibia
C150   schwantesii ssp. schwantesii var. schwantesii (kuibisensis)/25 km e Aus, Namibia
C151   lesliei ssp. lesliei var. lesliei (grey form)/25 km nw Christiana, SA
C152   lesliei ssp. lesliei var. mariae/30 km nne Kimberley, SA
C153   lesliei ssp. lesliei var. venteri (maraisii)/60 km nw Kimberley, SA
C154   hookeri var. marginata (red-brown form)/30 km nw Hopetown, SA
C155   hookeri var. marginata (red-brown form)/30 km nw Hopetown, SA
C156   hookeri var. subfenestrata/5 km n Prieska, SA
C157   verruculosa var. verruculosa (inae)/55 km ene Vanwyksvlei, SA
C158   hallii var. hallii/55 km ene Vanwyksvlei, SA
C159   verruculosa var. verruculosa/30 km ene Vanwyksvlei, SA
C160   verruculosa var. glabra/20 km sse Kenhardt, SA
C161   julii ssp. fulleri var. fulleri/near Pofadder, SA
C162A   julii ssp. fulleri var. fulleri/70 km wsw Pofadder, SA
C162B   olivacea var. nebrownii/70 km wsw Pofadder, SA
C163   marmorata var. marmorata/25 km ne Steinkopf, SA
C164   schwantesii ssp. schwantesii var. schwantesii/25 km sw Helmeringhausen, Namibia
C165   schwantesii ssp. gebseri/70 km s Maltahöhe, Namibia
C166   vallis-mariae/110 km nne Keetmanshoop, Namibia
C167   vallis-mariae (margarethae)/near Berseba, Namibia
C168   karasmontana ssp. + var. karasmont.(mickbergensis "summitatum")/10 km nne Grünau, Nam.
C169   karasmontana ssp. + var. karasmontana (mickbergensis)/20 km nne Grünau, Namibia
C170   fulviceps var. fulviceps/40 km n Karasburg, Namibia
C171   julii ssp. fulleri var. fulleri/60 km w Upington, SA
C172   aucampiae ssp. aucampiae var. aucampiae/5 km w Sishen, SA
C173   aucampiae ssp. aucampiae var. aucampiae (Kuruman form)/60 km se Kuruman, SA
C174   hallii var. hallii/25 km se Prieska, SA
C175   hookeri var. subfenestrata/ 20 km sse Prieska, SA
C176   hallii var. hallii/20 km se Prieska, SA
C177   verruculosa var. glabra/25 km sse Kenhardt, SA
C178   verruculosa var. verruculosa/90 km w Kenhardt, SA
C179   julii ssp. fulleri var. brunnea/10 km ne Pofadder, SA
C180   dinteri ssp. frederici/30 km nw Pofadder, SA
C181   dinteri ssp. multipunctata/65 km se Warmbad, Namibia
C182   karasmontana ssp. karasmontana var. tischeri/30 km nne Grünau, Namibia
C183   julii ssp. julii/25 km se Warmbad, Namibia
C184   schwantesii ssp. + var. schwantesii (gulielmi)/10 km nw Helmeringhausen, Namibia
C185   schwantesii ssp. schwantesii var. schwantesii/near Helmeringhausen, Namibia
C186   schwantesii ssp. schwant. var. urikosensis (kunjasensis)/5 km ne Helmeringhausen, Namibia
C187   pseudotruncatella ssp. pseudotruncatella var. elisabethiae/55 km ese Otjiwarongo, Namibia
C188   werneri/25 km nne Usakos, Namibia

C189   gracilidelineata ssp. gracilidelineata var. waldroniae/60 km se Swakopmund, Namibia
C189A   gracilidelineata ssp. grac. var. waldroniae acf Fritz´s White Lady/60 km se Swkpmd., Namibia
C190   schwantesii ssp. schwantesii var. schwantesii/70 km sw Maltahöhe, Namibia
C191   schwantesii ssp. schwantesii var. schwantesii/60 km nw Helmeringhausen, Namibia
C192   schwantesii ssp. schwantesii var. rugosa/40 km nw Helmeringhausen, Namibia
C193   karasmontana ssp. karasmontana var. lericheana/50 km nne Grünau, Namibia
C194   villetii ssp. villetii/60 km nnw Loeriesfontein, SA
C195   villetii ssp. villetii/30 km nne Loeriesfontein, SA
C196   verruculosa var. verruculosa (inae)/85 km s Pofadder, SA
C197   villetii ssp. kennedyi/75 km s Pofader, SA
C198   verruculosa var. verruculosa/85 km sse Pofadder, SA
C199   villetii ssp. kennedyi/75 km sse Pofadder, SA
C200A   villetii ssp. kennedyi/80 km sse Pofadder, SA
C200B   verruculosa var. verruculosa/80 km sse Pofadder, SA
C201   divergens var. amethystina/60 km wnw Loeriesfontein, SA
C202   divergens var. divergens/35 km nnw Vanrhynsdorp, SA
C203   julii ssp. fulleri var. fulleri/15 km sse Kenhardt, SA
C204   lesliei ssp. lesliei var. rubrobrunnea/5 km nw Krugersdorp, SA
C205   julii ssp. julii (chrysocephala)/50 km se Warmbad, Namibia
C206   dinteri ssp. dinteri var. dinteri/40 km sse Warmbad, Namibia
C206A   dinteri ssp. dinteri var. dinteri acf Dintergreen/40 km sse Warmbad, Namibia
C207   gesinae var. gesinae/70 km n Aus, Namibia
C208   karasmontana ssp. eberlanzii/10 km s Aus, Namibia
C209   karasmontana ssp. eberlanzii (erniana)/10 km sse Aus, Namibia
C210   schwantesii ssp. schwantesii var. urikosensis (christinae)/45 km w Maltahöhe, Namibia
C211   schwantesii ssp. schwantesii var. schwantesii/10 km se Helmeringhausen, Namibia
C212   meyeri/40 km nne Port Nolloth, SA
C213   herrei /65 km ne Alexander Bay, SA
C214   marmorata var. elisae/35 km se Vioolsdrif, SA
C215   julii ssp. fulleri var. rouxii/75 km wsw Warmbad, Namibia
C216   julii ssp. fulleri var. rouxii/60 km wsw Warmbad, Namibia
C217   julii ssp. fulleri var. rouxii/70 km wsw Warmbad, Namibia
C218   julii ssp. julii (littlewoodii)/40 km wsw Warmbad, Namibia
C219   fulviceps var. fulviceps (lydiae)/60 km n Karasburg, Namibia
C220   fulviceps var. fulviceps/75 km n Karasburg, Namibia
C221   fulviceps var. fulviceps/85 km n Karasburg, Namibia
C222   fulviceps var. lactinea/100 km ese Keetmanshoop, Namibia
C223   karasmontana ssp. karasmontana var. karasmontana/25 km ne Grünau, Namibia
C224   karasmontana ssp. karasmontana var. aiaisensis/110 km w Karasburg, Namibia
C225   karasmontana ssp. karasmontana var. karasmontana/30 km nw Grünau, Namibia
C226   karasmontana ssp. karasmontana var. karasmontana/25 km w Grünau, Namibia
C227   karasmontana ssp. karasm. var. karasmontana (jacobseniana)/10 km sw Grünau, Namibia
C228   villetii ssp. kennedyi/90 km s Pofadder, SA
C229A   villetii ssp. kennedyi/90 km s Pofadder, SA
C229B   verruculosa var. verruculosa/90 km s Pofadder, SA
C230A   villetii ssp. deboeri/75 km e Gamoep, SA
C230B   julii ssp. fulleri var. fulleri/75 km e Gamoep, SA
C230C   verruculosa var. verruculosa/75 km e Gamoep, SA
C231   villetii ssp. deboeri/75 km e Gamoep, SA
C232   geyeri (hillii)/65 km ne Port Nolloth, SA
C233   geyeri (hillii)/65 km Port Nolloth, SA
C234   herrei/70 km ne Alexander Bay, SA
C235   herrei//35 km ne Alexander Bay, SA
C236   herrei (translucens)/15 km ne Alexander Bay, SA
C237   herrei (translucens)/15 km e Alexander Bay, SA
C238   vallis-mariae/85 km ne Keetmanshoop, Namibia

C239   pseudotruncatella ssp. groendrayensis/45 km sse Rehoboth, Namibia
C240   ruschiorum var. ruschiorum (nelii)/ 25 km e Cape Cross/Kaap Kruis, Namibia
C241   ruschiorum var. ruschiorum/65 km ene Henties Bay, Namibia
C242   ruschiorum var. ruschiorum/65 km ene Swakopmund, Namibia
C243   gracilidelineata ssp. gracilidelineata var. waldroniae/70 km e Swakopmund, Namibia
C244   pseudotruncatella ssp. groendrayensis/50 km s Rehoboth, Namibia
C245   pseudotruncatella ssp. dendritica (farinosa)/55 km ssw Rehoboth, Namibia
C246   pseudotruncatella ssp. groendrayensis(Witkop form)/55 km s Rehoboth, Namibia
C247   schwantesii ssp. schwantesii var. rugosa/40 km nw Helmeringhausen, Namibia
C248   schwantesii ssp. schwant. var. urikosensis (kunjasensis)/15 km ne Helmeringhausen, Namibia
C249   schwantesii ssp. schwantesii var. marthae/60 km sse Aus, Namibia
C250   schwantesii ssp. schwantesii var. schwantesii (grey form)/120 km se Aus, Namibia
C251   marmorata var. elisae/30 km se Vioolsdrif, SA
C252   marmorata var. elisae/30 km sse Vioolsdrif, SA
C253   terricolor (peersii)/ 95 km nw Port Elizabeth, SA
C254   terricolor (peersii)/30 km ene Willowmore, SA
C255   aucampiae ssp. aucampiae var. aucampiae/15 km nnw Postmasburg, SA
C256   aucampiae ssp. aucampiae var. koelemanii/35 km wsw Postmasburg, SA
C257   aucampiae ssp. aucampiae var. aucampiae/40 km w Postmasburg, SA
C258   villetii ssp. deboeri/35 km ene Gamoep, SA
C259   julii ssp. fulleri var. fulleri/40 km ene Gamoep, SA
C260   marmorata var. marmorata (diutina)/15 km ene Steinkopf, SA
C261   gracilidelineata ssp. gracilidelineata var. gracilidelineata/75 km nw Usakos, Namibia
C262   gracilidelineata ssp. gracilidelineata var. gracilidelineata/30 km nw Usakos, Namibia
C263   pseudotruncatella ssp. pseudotruncatella var. pseudotruncatella/20 km w Windhoek, Namibia
C264   pseudotruncatella ssp. + var. pseudotrunc. (pallid form)/60 km ssw Windhoek, Namibia
C265   schwantesii ssp. schwantesii var. schwantesii/45 km n Helmeringhausen, Namibia
C266   fulviceps var. fulviceps/65 km n Karasburg, Namibia
C267   karasmontana ssp. karasmontana var. lericheana/70 km n Karasburg, Namibia
C268   dinteri ssp. dinteri var. brevis/55 km sw Warmbad, Namibia
C269   divergens var. divergens/10 km ne Bitterfontein, SA
C270   divergens var. amethystina/80 km wnw Loeriesfontein, SA
C271   helmutii/15 km ne Steinkopf, SA
C272   meyeri/45 km nne Port Nolloth, SA
C272A   meyeri acf Hammeruby/45 km nne Port Nolloth, SA
C273   meyeri/55 km nne Port Nolloth, SA
C274   geyeri/75 km ene Alexander Bay, SA
C275   optica/10 km n Lüderitz, Namibia
C276   optica/10 km s Lüderitz, Namibia
C277   optica/10 km sw Lüderitz, Namibia
C278   fulviceps var. fulviceps/70 km w Upington, Namibia
C279   bromfieldii var. bromfieldii/45 km e Upington, SA
C280   otzeniana/45 km nnw Loeriesfontein, SA
C281   vallis-mariae/15 km e Mariental, Namibia
C282   vallis-mariae/ 125 km n Keetmanshoop, Namibia
C283   bromfieldii var. mennellii/20 km ssw Upington, SA
C284   fulviceps var. fulviceps/15 km ne Karasburg, Namibia
C285   karasmontana ssp. bella/near Aus, Namibia
C286   optica/10 km sw Lüderitz, Namibia
C287   optica cv. Rubra/10 km sw Lüderitz, Namibia
C288   optica/40 km sse Lüderitz, Namibia
C289   optica/50 km s Lüderitz, Namibia
C290   optica/65 km s Lüderitz, Namibia
C291   optica (maculate form)/100 km sse Lüderitz, Namibia
C292   optica/120 km sse Lüderitz, Namibia
C293   optica (maculate form)/ 95 km sse Lüderitz, Namibia

C294   optica/140 km sse Lüderitz, Namibia
C295   karasmontana ssp. bella/115 km sse Aus, Namibia
C296   vallis-mariae/40 km sse Koes; Namibia
C297   julii ssp. julii/45 km se Warmbad, Namibia
C297A   julii ssp. julii acf Peppermint Créme/45 km se Warmbad, Namibia
C298   aucampiae ssp. aucampiae var. aucampiae/near Severn/120 km nnw Kuruman, SA
C299   schwantesii ssp. schwantesii var. marthae, 120 km sse Aus, Namibia
C300   dorotheae/15 km n Pofadder, SA
C301   hookeri var. dabneri/20 km nne Douglas, SA
C302   lesliei ssp. burchellii/20 km nne Douglas, SA
C303   hallii var. ochracea/30 km e Kenhardt, SA
C304   naureeniae/60 km se Springbok, SA
C305   marmorata var. marmorata/40 km nne Steinkopf, SA
C306   pseudotruncatella ssp. archerae/120 km nw Maltahöhe, Namibia
C307   optica/170 km sse Lüderitz, Namibia
C308   lesliei ssp. burchelli/10 km nne Douglas, SA
C309   gracilidelineata ssp. gracilidelineata var. gracilidelineata/45 km w Usakos, Namibia
C310   optica/160 km sse Lüderitz, Namibia
C311   optica (maculate form)/ 45 km se Lüderitz, Namibia
C312   ruschiorum var. lineata/50 km ne Rocky Point, Namibia
C313   ruschiorum var. lineata/45 km n Rocky Point, Namibia
C314   ruschiorum var. lineata/40 km ne Cape Fria, Namibia
C315   pseudotruncatella ssp. pseudotruncatella var. pseudotruncatella/20 km ene Windhoek, Namibia
C316   ruschiorum var. ruschiorum (nelii)/near Cape Cross/Kaap Kruis, Namibia
C317   karasmontana ssp. + var. karasmontana (mickbergensis)/15 km nne Grünau, Namibia
C318   hallii var. hallii/45 km ssw Prieska, SA
C319   julii ssp. fulleri var. fulleri/5 km ne Pofadder, SA
C320   salicola/10 km wnw Luckhoff, SA
C321   salicola/25 km wnw Petrusville, SA
C322   salicola/20 km sw Luckhoff, SA
C323   julii ssp. fulleri var. fulleri/25 km sw Upington, SA
C324   julii ssp. fulleri var. rouxii/55 km w Warmbad, Namibia
C325   aucampiae ssp. aucampiae var. aucampiae (Kuruman form)/10 km w Reivilo, SA
C326   dinteri ssp. multipunctata/65 km se Warmbad, Namibia
C327   karasmontana ssp. + var. karasmontana (mickbergensis)/15 km nne Grünau, Namibia
C328   karasmontana ssp. + var. karasmontana (Signalberg form)/25 km wnw Grünau, Namibia
C329   karasmontana ssp. karasmontana var. lericheana/70 km n Karasburg, Namibia
C330   karasmontana ssp. karasmontana var. lericheana/70 km n Karasburg, Namibia
C331   lesliei ssp. lesliei var. lesliei/15 km sse Pretoria, SA
C332   aucampiae ssp. aucampiae var. aucampiae (Kuruman form)/5 km ne Kuruman, SA
C333   aucampiae ssp. aucampiae var. aucampiae/near Griquatown/Griekwastad, SA
C334   aucampiae ssp. aucampiae var. aucampiae/15 km nne Olifantshoek, SA
C335   hookeri var. hookeri (vermiculate form)/30 km wsw Strydenburg, SA
C336   hookeri var. hookeri (vermiculate form)/ 45 km ssw Prieska, SA
C337   hookeri var. marginata (red-brown form)/30 km se Douglas, SA
C338   hookeri var. marginata/35 km se Hopetown, SA
C339   terricolor (peersii)/near Steytlerville, SA
C340   hookeri var. hookeri/near Marydale, SA
C341   lesliei ssp. lesliei var. lesliei (Kimberley form)/ 20 km nw Kimberley, SA
C342   lesliei ssp. lesliei var. lesliei/10 km ne Pretoria, SA
C343   lesliei ssp. lesliei var. lesliei/near Vanderbylpark, SA
C344   lesliei ssp. lesliei var. lesliei/near Orkney, SA
C345   terricolor/30 km wnw Prince Albert Road, SA
C345A   terricolor acf Speckled Gold/30 km wnw Prince Albert Road, SA
C346   terricolor/30 km wnw Prince Albert Road, SA
C347   comptonii var. weberi/70 km ssw Calvinia, SA

C348   bromfieldii var. bromfieldii/20 km e Upington, SA
C349   julii ssp. julii/45 km se Warmbad, Namibia
C350   otzeniana/40 km nnw Loeriesfontein, SA
C351   salicola/10 km w Luckhoff, SA
C351A   salicola acf Malachite/10 km w Luckhoff, SA
C352   lesliei ssp. lesliei var. lesliei/45 km e Pietersburg, SA
C353   salicola/15 km wnw Luckhoff, SA
C354   lesliei ssp. lesliei var. lesliei (Kimberley form)/15 km nw Kimberley, SA
C355   herrei/65 km nne Oranjemund, Namibia
C356   divergens var. amethystina/45 km nw Loeriesfontein, SA
C357   pseudotruncatella ssp. dendritica/75 km sw Rehoboth, Namibia
C358   lesliei ssp. lesliei var. lesliei/25 km w Lobatse, Botswana
C359   lesliei ssp. lesliei var. lesliei (grey form)/115 km sw Lobatse, Botswana
C360   marmorata var. marmorata/35 km ne Steinkopf, SA
C361   herrei/30 km ne Alexander Bay, SA
C362   bromfieldii var. insularis acf Sulphurea/unknown
C363   fulviceps var. fulviceps acf Aurea/unknown
C364   lesliei ssp. lesliei var. hornii/45 km ssw Kimberley, SA
C365   marmorata var. marmorata (framesii)/60 km ne Springbok, SA
C366   aucampiae ssp. aucampiae var. aucampiae/near Danielskuil, SA
C367   gracilidelineata ssp. gracilidelineata var. gracilidelineata/150 km nw Usakos, Namibia
C368   bromfieldii var. bromfieldii/25 km se Upington, SA
C369   karasmontana ssp. eberlanzii/20 km e Lüderitz, Namibia
C370   karasmontana ssp. eberlanzii/35 km e Lüderitz, Namibia
C370A   karasmontana ssp. eberlanzii acf Avocado Cream/35 km e Lüderitz, Namibia
C371   francisci/35 km e Lüderitz, Namibia
C372   hallii var. ochracea/15 km sw Upington, SA
C373   gracilidelineata ssp. + var. gracilidelineata (streyi)/25 km se Franzfontein, Namibia
C374   gracilidelineata ssp. + var. gracilidelineata/100 km s Usakos, Namibia
C375   hallii var. hallii/55 km n Upington, SA
C376   terricolor (peersii)/35 km ese Willowmore, SA
C377   comptonii var. comptonii/70 km ne Ceres, SA
C378   julii ssp. fulleri var. fulleri/65 km ne Springbok, SA
C379   terricolor/60 km e Prince Albert, SA
C380   ruschiorum var. lineata/50 km ene Rocky Point, Namibia
C381   pseudotruncatella ssp. + var. pseudotruncatella (alpina)/ 30 km s Windhoek, Namibia
C382   bromfieldii var. glaudinae/70 km w Griquatown/Griekwastad, SA
C383   gracilidelineata ssp. brandbergensis/Brandberg, Namibia
C384   pseudotruncatella ssp. dendritica/6 km s Rehoboth, Namibia
C385   gracilidelineata ssp. gracilidelineata var. gracilidelineata/65 km e Swakopmund, Namibia
C385A   gracilidelineata ssp. + var. grac. acf Ernst's Witkop/65 km ene Swakopmund, Namibia
C386   ruschiorum var. lineata/40 km nne Rocky Point, Namibia
C387   ruschiorum var. ruschiorum/8 km n Rössing, Namibia
C387A   ruschiorum var. ruschiorum acf Silver Reed/8 km n Rössing, Namibia
C388   steineckeana/habitat unknown; hybrid?
C389   aucampiae ssp. aucampiae var. aucampiae acf Betty's Beryl, unknown
C390   fulviceps var. fulviceps/30 km nw Grünau, Namibia
C391   fulviceps var. fulviceps/25 km nw Grünau, Namibia
C392   aucampiae ssp. aucampiae var. aucampiae acf Storms's Snowcap, unknown
C393   bromfieldii var. glaudinae/70 km wnw Griquatown/Griekwastad, SA
C394   gracilidelineata ssp. brandbergensis/Brandberg, Namibia
C395   aucampiae ssp. aucampiae var. aucampiae acf Jackson's Jade, unknown
C396   coleorum/near Ellisras, SA
C397   hermetica/Sperrgebiet, Tsaus Plateau, 140 km se Lüderitz, Namibia
C397A   hermetica acf Green Diamond/Sperrgebiet, Tsaus Plateau, 140km se Lüderitz, Namibia
C398   karasmontana ssp. eberlanzii/45 km e Lüderitz, Namibia

C399   karasmontana ssp. eberlanzii/45 km e Lüderitz, Namibia
C400   karasmontana ssp. eberlanzii/45 km e Lüderitz, Namibia
C401   karasmontana ssp. eberlanzii/25 km se Lüderitz, Namibia
C402   karasmontana ssp. eberlanzii acf Avocado Cream/40 km e Lüderitz, Namibia
C403   olivacea var. nebrownii/near Aggeneys, SA
C404   optica/Sperrgebiet, 15 km n Bogenfels, Namibia
C405   karasmontana ssp. eberlanzii/50 km e Lüderitz, Namibia
C406   gesinae var. gesinae/80 km ssw Maltahöhe, Namibia
C407   lesliei ssp. lesliei var. lesliei/15 km n Krugersdorp, SA
C408   karasmontana ssp. karasmontana var. karasmontana/40 km ne Ai-Ais, Namibia
C409   karasmontana ssp. karasmontana var. aiaisensis/30 km e Ai-Ais, Namibia
C410   amicorum/75 km se Aus, Namibia
C411   schwantesii ssp. schwantesii var. marthae/75 km se Aus, Namibia
C412   fulviceps var. laevigata/90 km ne Pofadder, SA
C413   pseudotruncatella ssp. + var. pseudotruncatella/100 km w Windhoek, Namibia
C414   optica/around Lüderitz Bay, Namibia
C415   fulviceps var. fulviceps (pale form)/near Fish River Canyon, Namibia
C416   julii ssp. fulleri var. fulleri/e of Onseepkans, SA
C417   karasmontana ssp. karasmontana var. immaculata/10 km n Grünau, Namibia
C418   terricolor/ne Willowmore, SA
C419   meyeri/45 km nne Port Nolloth, SA
C420   hookeri var. hookeri/50 km sw Hopetown, SA

Lithops bromfieldii var. insularis acf Sulphurea C362

Cole Fieldnumberlist Lithops (alphabetical order)

C410   amicorum/75 km se Aus, Namibia

C012   aucampiae ssp. aucampiae var. aucampiae (Kuruman form)/10 km e Kuruman, SA
C325   aucampiae ssp. aucampiae var. aucampiae (Kuruman form)/10 km w Reivilo, SA
C332   aucampiae ssp. aucampiae var. aucampiae (Kuruman form)/5 km ne Kuruman, SA
C011   aucampiae ssp. aucampiae var. aucampiae (Kuruman form)/5 km sw Kuruman, SA
C173   aucampiae ssp. aucampiae var. aucampiae (Kuruman form)/60 km se Kuruman, SA
C395   aucampiae ssp. aucampiae var. aucampiae acf Jackson's Jade, unknown
C392   aucampiae ssp. aucampiae var. aucampiae acf Storms's Snowcap, unknown
C389   aucampiae ssp. aucampiae var. aucampiae acf Betty's Beryl, unknown
C003   aucampiae ssp. aucampiae var. aucampiae/10km se Postmasburg, SA
C334   aucampiae ssp. aucampiae var. aucampiae/15 km nne Olifantshoek, SA
C255   aucampiae ssp. aucampiae var. aucampiae/15 km nnw Postmasburg, SA
C257   aucampiae ssp. aucampiae var. aucampiae/40 km w Postmasburg, SA
C117   aucampiae ssp. aucampiae var. aucampiae/45 km nw Griquatown/Griekwastad, SA
C004   aucampiae ssp. aucampiae var. aucampiae/5 km n Postmasburg, SA
C046   aucampiae ssp. aucampiae var. aucampiae/5 km ne Griquatown/Griekwastad, SA
C172   aucampiae ssp. aucampiae var. aucampiae/5 km w Sishen, SA
C061   aucampiae ssp. aucampiae var. aucampiae/70 km wsw Vryburg, SA
C002   aucampiae ssp. aucampiae var. aucampiae/near Danielskuil, SA
C366   aucampiae ssp. aucampiae var. aucampiae/near Danielskuil, SA
C333   aucampiae ssp. aucampiae var. aucampiae/near Griquatown/Griekwastad, SA
C298   aucampiae ssp. aucampiae var. aucampiae/near Severn/120 km nnw Kuruman, SA
C016   aucampiae ssp. aucampiae var. koelemanii/35 km nw Postmasburg, SA
C256   aucampiae ssp. aucampiae var. koelemanii/35 km wsw Postmasburg, SA
C048   aucampiae ssp. euniceae var. euniceae/15 km n Hopetown, SA
C054   aucampiae ssp. euniceae var. fluminalis/near Hopetown, SA

C382   bromfieldii var. glaudinae/70 km w Griquatown/Griekwastad, SA
C040   bromfieldii var. bromfieldii/15 km ene Upington, SA
C041   bromfieldii var. bromfieldii/15 km ene Upington, SA
C348   bromfieldii var. bromfieldii/20 km e Upington, SA
C368   bromfieldii var. bromfieldii/25 km se Upington, SA
C279   bromfieldii var. bromfieldii/45 km e Upington, SA
C116   bromfieldii var. glaudinae/70 km wnw Griquatown/Griekwastad, SA
C393   bromfieldii var. glaudinae/70 km wnw Griquatown/Griekwastad, SA
C362   bromfieldii var. insularis acf Sulphurea/unknown
C057   bromfieldii var. insularis/10 km ne Keimoes, SA
C042   bromfieldii var. insularis/15 km e Keimoes, SA
C043   bromfieldii var. insularis/15 km e Keimoes, SA
C283   bromfieldii var. mennellii/20 km ssw Upington, SA
C044   bromfieldii var. mennellii/25 km ssw Upington, SA

C396   coleorum/near Ellisras, SA

C125   comptonii var. comptonii/50 km ene Ceres, SA
C377   comptonii var. comptonii/70 km ne Ceres, SA
C126   comptonii var. weberi/70 km s Calvinia, SA
C347   comptonii var. weberi/70 km ssw Calvinia, SA

C084   dinteri ssp. dinteri var. brevis/20 km se Vioolsdrif, SA

C268   dinteri ssp. dinteri var. brevis/55 km sw Warmbad, Namibia
C206A   dinteri ssp. dinteri var. dinteri acf Dintergreen/40 km sse Warmbad, Namibia
C206   dinteri ssp. dinteri var. dinteri/40 km sse Warmbad, Namibia
C180   dinteri ssp. frederici/30 km nw Pofadder, SA
C181   dinteri ssp. multipunctata/65 km se Warmbad, Namibia
C326   dinteri ssp. multipunctata/65 km se Warmbad, Namibia

C356   divergens var. amethystina/45 km nw Loeriesfontein, SA
C201   divergens var. amethystina/60 km wnw Loeriesfontein, SA
C270   divergens var. amethystina/80 km wnw Loeriesfontein, SA
C269   divergens var. divergens/10 km ne Bitterfontein, SA
C202   divergens var. divergens/35 km nnw Vanrhynsdorp, SA

C124   dorotheae/15 km n Pofadder, SA
C300   dorotheae/15 km n Pofadder, SA

C140   francisci/35 km e Lüderitz, Namibia
C371   francisci/35 km e Lüderitz, Namibia

C219   fulviceps var. fulviceps (lydiae)/60 km n Karasburg, Namibia
C363   fulviceps var. fulviceps acf Aurea/unknown
C284   fulviceps var. fulviceps/15 km ne Karasburg, Namibia
C391   fulviceps var. fulviceps/25 km nw Grünau, Namibia
C390   fulviceps var. fulviceps/30 km nw Grünau, Namibia
C170   fulviceps var. fulviceps/40 km n Karasburg, Namibia
C266   fulviceps var. fulviceps/65 km n Karasburg, Namibia
C278   fulviceps var. fulviceps/70 km w Upington, Namibia
C220   fulviceps var. fulviceps/75 km n Karasburg, Namibia
C221   fulviceps var. fulviceps/85 km n Karasburg, Namibia
C415   fulviceps var. fulviceps (pale form)/near Fish River Canyon
C222   fulviceps var. lactinea/100 km ese Keetmanshoop, Namibia
C412   fulviceps var. laevigata/90 km ne Pofadder, SA

C078   gesinae var. annae/25 km sw Helmeringhausen, Namibia
C207   gesinae var. gesinae/70 km n Aus, Namibia
C406   gesinae var. gesinae/80 km ssw Maltahöhe, Namibia

C232   geyeri (hillii)/65 km ne Port Nolloth, SA
C233   geyeri (hillii)/65 km Port Nolloth, SA
C274   geyeri/75 km ene Alexander Bay, SA

C385A   gracilidelineata ssp. + var. grac. acf Ernst´s Witkop/65 km ene Swakopmund, Namibia
C373   gracilidelineata ssp. + var. gracilidelineata (streyi)/25 km se Franzfontein, Namibia
C374   gracilidelineata ssp. + var. gracilidelineata/100 km s Usakos, Namibia
C383   gracilidelineata ssp. brandbergensis/Brandberg, Namibia
C394   gracilidelineata ssp. brandbergensis/Brandberg, Namibia
C189A   gracilidelineata ssp. grac. var. waldroniae acf Fritz´s White Lady/60 km se Swkpmd., Namibia
C367   gracilidelineata ssp. gracilidelineata var. gracilidelineata/150 km nw Usakos, Namibia
C262   gracilidelineata ssp. gracilidelineata var. gracilidelineata/30 km nw Usakos, Namibia
C309   gracilidelineata ssp. gracilidelineata var. gracilidelineata/45 km w Usakos, Namibia
C385   gracilidelineata ssp. gracilidelineata var. gracilidelineata/65 km e Swakopmund, Namibia
C261   gracilidelineata ssp. gracilidelineata var. gracilidelineata/75 km nw Usakos, Namibia
C189   gracilidelineata ssp. gracilidelineata var. waldroniae/60 km se Swakopmund, Namibia
C243   gracilidelineata ssp. gracilidelineata var. waldroniae/70 km e Swakopmund, Namibia

C135   hallii var. hallii (brown form)/20 km se Strydenburg, SA
C136   hallii var. hallii (brown form)/35 km ene Strydenburg, SA

C119   hallii var. hallii (grey form)/30 km wsw Strydenburg, SA
C087   hallii var. hallii (salicola reticulata)/30 km se Hopetown, SA
C050   hallii var. hallii/15 km se Strydenburg, SA
C045   hallii var. hallii/15 km sw Upington, SA
C176   hallii var. hallii/20 km se Prieska, SA
C174   hallii var. hallii/25 km se Prieska, SA
C052   hallii var. hallii/25 km sse Hopetown, SA
C094   hallii var. hallii/45 km se Prieska, SA
C318   hallii var. hallii/45 km ssw Prieska, SA
C090   hallii var. hallii/50 km nw Hopetown, SA
C158   hallii var. hallii/55 km ene Vanwyksvlei, SA
C375   hallii var. hallii/55 km n Upington, SA
C022   hallii var. hallii/55 km sw Prieska, SA
C111A   hallii var. ochracea acf Green Soapstone/35 km wnw Prieska, SA
C059   hallii var. ochracea/10 km nw Upington, SA
C372   hallii var. ochracea/15 km sw Upington, SA
C303   hallii var. ochracea/30 km e Kenhardt, SA
C142A   hallii var. ochracea/30 km nw Niekerkshoop, SA
C111   hallii var. ochracea/35 km wnw Prieska, SA
C039   hallii var. ochracea/5 km ne Groblershoop, SA
C098   hallii var. ochracea/50 km nnw Upington, SA

C271   helmutii/15 km ne Steinkopf, SA

C397A   hermetica acf Green Diamond/Sperrgebiet, Tsaus Plateau, 140km se Lüderitz, Namibia
C397   hermetica/Sperrgebiet, Tsaus Plateau, 140 km se Lüderitz, Namibia

C237   herrei (translucens)/15 km e Alexander Bay, SA
C236   herrei (translucens)/15 km ne Alexander Bay, SA
C213   herrei /65 km ne Alexander Bay, SA
C235   herrei//35 km ne Alexander Bay, SA
C361   herrei/30 km ne Alexander Bay, SA
C355   herrei/65 km nne Oranjemund, Namibia
C234   herrei/70 km ne Alexander Bay, SA

C301   hookeri var. dabneri/20 km nne Douglas, SA
C013   hookeri var. dabneri/25 km s Kimberley, SA
C085   hookeri var. dabneri/35 km w Kimberley, SA
C092   hookeri var. elephina/10 km n Britstown, SA
C093   hookeri var. elephina/25 km ne Britstown, SA
C336   hookeri var. hookeri (vermiculate form)/ 45 km ssw Prieska, SA
C051   hookeri var. hookeri (vermiculate form)/15 km nw Strydenburg, SA
C335   hookeri var. hookeri (vermiculate form)/30 km wsw Strydenburg, SA
C023   hookeri var. hookeri (vermiculate form)/55 km sw Prieska, SA
C113   hookeri var. hookeri/10 km nw Niekerkshoop, SA
C114   hookeri var. hookeri/15 km nw Niekerkshoop, SA
C118   hookeri var. hookeri/25 km w Strydenburg, SA
C142B   hookeri var. hookeri/30 km nw Niekerkshoop, SA
C112   hookeri var. hookeri/40 km wnw Prieska, SA
C110   hookeri var. hookeri/50 km nw Marydale, SA
C340   hookeri var. hookeri/near Marydale, SA
C038   hookeri var. lutea/5 km ne Groblershoop, SA
C088   hookeri var. marginata (cerise form)/20 km ene Hopetown, SA
C089   hookeri var. marginata (red-brown form)/25 km nw Hopetown, SA
C053   hookeri var. marginata (red-brown form)/25 km sw Douglas, SA
C154   hookeri var. marginata (red-brown form)/30 km nw Hopetown, SA

C155   hookeri var. marginata (red-brown form)/30 km nw Hopetown, SA
C337   hookeri var. marginata (red-brown form)/30 km se Douglas, SA
C035   hookeri var. marginata/25 km se Hopetown, SA
C137   hookeri var. marginata/35 km e Hopetown, SA
C338   hookeri var. marginata/35 km se Hopetown, SA
C420   hookeri var. hookeri/50 km sw Hopetown, SA
C019   hookeri var. subfenestrata (brunneoviolacea)/40 km sw Griquatown/Griekwastad, SA
C175   hookeri var. subfenestrata/ 20 km sse Prieska, SA
C021   hookeri var. subfenestrata/15 km ssw Prieska, SA
C156   hookeri var. subfenestrata/5 km n Prieska, SA
C091   hookeri var. susannae/30 km se Douglas, SA

C179   julii ssp. fulleri var. brunnea/10 km ne Pofadder, SA
C056A   julii ssp. fulleri var. fulleri acf Fullergreen/25 km sw Pofadder, SA
C121   julii ssp. fulleri var. fulleri/115 km w Kenhardt, SA
C122   julii ssp. fulleri var. fulleri/125 km w Kenhardt, SA
C203   julii ssp. fulleri var. fulleri/15 km sse Kenhardt, SA
C056   julii ssp. fulleri var. fulleri/25 km sw Pofadder, SA
C323   julii ssp. fulleri var. fulleri/25 km sw Upington, SA
C259   julii ssp. fulleri var. fulleri/40 km ene Gamoep, SA
C024   julii ssp. fulleri var. fulleri/5 km n Kenhardt, SA
C319   julii ssp. fulleri var. fulleri/5 km ne Pofadder, SA
C171   julii ssp. fulleri var. fulleri/60 km w Upington, SA
C378   julii ssp. fulleri var. fulleri/65 km ne Springbok, SA
C162A   julii ssp. fulleri var. fulleri/70 km wsw Pofadder, SA
C230B   julii ssp. fulleri var. fulleri/75 km e Gamoep, SA
C062   julii ssp. fulleri var. fulleri/near Kakamas, SA
C161   julii ssp. fulleri var. fulleri/near Pofadder, SA
C416   Julii ssp. Fulleri var. fulleri/e of Onseepkans, SA
C324   julii ssp. fulleri var. rouxii/55 km w Warmbad, Namibia
C216   julii ssp. fulleri var. rouxii/60 km wsw Warmbad, Namibia
C217   julii ssp. fulleri var. rouxii/70 km wsw Warmbad, Namibia
C215   julii ssp. fulleri var. rouxii/75 km wsw Warmbad, Namibia
C205   julii ssp. julii (chrysocephala)/50 km se Warmbad, Namibia
C218   julii ssp. julii (littlewoodii)/40 km wsw Warmbad, Namibia
C297A   julii ssp. julii acf Peppermint Créme/45 km se Warmbad, Namibia
C183   julii ssp. julii/25 km se Warmbad, Namibia
C297   julii ssp. julii/45 km se Warmbad, Namibia
C349   julii ssp. julii/45 km se Warmbad, Namibia
C063   julii ssp. julii/60 km se Warmbad, Namibia
C064   julii ssp. julii/near Karasburg, Namibia

C168   karasmontana ssp. + var. karasmont.(mickbergensis "summitatum")/10 km nne Grünau, Nam.
C317   karasmontana ssp. + var. karasmontana (mickbergensis)/15 km nne Grünau, Namibia
C327   karasmontana ssp. + var. karasmontana (mickbergensis)/15 km nne Grünau, Namibia
C169   karasmontana ssp. + var. karasmontana (mickbergensis)/20 km nne Grünau, Namibia
C065   karasmontana ssp. + var. karasmontana (Signalberg form)/25 km wnw Grünau, Namibia
C328   karasmontana ssp. + var. karasmontana (Signalberg form)/25 km wnw Grünau, Namibia
C295   karasmontana ssp. bella/115 km sse Aus, Namibia
C108   karasmontana ssp. bella/5 km s Aus, Namibia
C143A   karasmontana ssp. bella/60 km nne Aus, Namibia
C285   karasmontana ssp. bella/near Aus, Namibia
C149   karasmontana ssp. eberlanzii (erniana witputzensis)/110 km sse Aus, Namibia
C209   karasmontana ssp. eberlanzii (erniana)/10 km sse Aus, Namibia
C147   karasmontana ssp. eberlanzii (erniana)/40 km s Aus, Namibia
C370A   karasmontana ssp. eberlanzii acf Avocado Cream/35 km e Lüderitz, Namibia
C402   karasmontana ssp. eberlanzii acf Avocado Cream/40 km e Lüderitz, Namibia

C208   karasmontana ssp. eberlanzii/10 km s Aus, Namibia
C369   karasmontana ssp. eberlanzii/20 km e Lüderitz, Namibia
C401   karasmontana ssp. eberlanzii/25 km se Lüderitz, Namibia
C082   karasmontana ssp. eberlanzii/35 km e Lüderitz, Namibia
C370   karasmontana ssp. eberlanzii/35 km e Lüderitz, Namibia
C398   karasmontana ssp. eberlanzii/45 km e Lüderitz, Namibia
C399   karasmontana ssp. eberlanzii/45 km e Lüderitz, Namibia
C400   karasmontana ssp. eberlanzii/45 km e Lüderitz, Namibia
C405   karasmontana ssp. eberlanzii/50 km e Lüderitz, Namibia
C227   karasmontana ssp. karasm. var. karasmontana (jacobseniana)/10 km sw Grünau, Namibia
C224   karasmontana ssp. karasmontana var. aiaisensis/110 km w Karasburg, Namibia
C409   karasmontana ssp. karasmontana var. aiaisensis/30 km e Ai-Ais, Namibia
C417   karasmontana ssp. karasmontana var. immaculata/10 km n Grünau, Namibia
C223   karasmontana ssp. karasmontana var. karasmontana/25 km ne Grünau, Namibia
C226   karasmontana ssp. karasmontana var. karasmontana/25 km w Grünau, Namibia
C225   karasmontana ssp. karasmontana var. karasmontana/30 km nw Grünau, Namibia
C193   karasmontana ssp. karasmontana var. lericheana/50 km nne Grünau, Namibia
C267   karasmontana ssp. karasmontana var. lericheana/70 km n Karasburg, Namibia
C329   karasmontana ssp. karasmontana var. lericheana/70 km n Karasburg, Namibia
C330   karasmontana ssp. karasmontana var. lericheana/70 km n Karasburg, Namibia
C182   karasmontana ssp. karasmontana var. tischeri/30 km nne Grünau, Namibia
C408   karasmontana ssp. karasmontana var. karasmontana/40 km ne Ai-Ais, Namibia

C308   lesliei ssp. burchelli/10 km nne Douglas, SA
C302   lesliei ssp. burchellii/20 km nne Douglas, SA
C015   lesliei ssp. lesliei var. hornii/40 km sw Kimberley, SA
C364   lesliei ssp. lesliei var. hornii/45 km ssw Kimberley, SA
C359   lesliei ssp. lesliei var. lesliei (grey form)/115 km sw Lobatse, Botswana
C151   lesliei ssp. lesliei var. lesliei (grey form)/25 km nw Christiana, SA
C008   lesliei ssp. lesliei var. lesliei (grey form)/70 km w Mafikeng, SA
C009   lesliei ssp. lesliei var. lesliei (grey form)/70 km w Mafikeng, SA
C341   lesliei ssp. lesliei var. lesliei (Kimberley form)/ 20 km nw Kimberley, SA
C014   lesliei ssp. lesliei var. lesliei (Kimberley form)/15 km nw Kimberley, SA
C354   lesliei ssp. lesliei var. lesliei (Kimberley form)/15 km nw Kimberley, SA
C020   lesliei ssp. lesliei var. lesliei (luteoviridis)/15 km w Magaliesburg, SA
C032   lesliei ssp. lesliei var. lesliei (Pietersburg form)/10 km se Pietersburg, SA
C030   lesliei ssp. lesliei var. lesliei (Pietersburg form)/30 km nw Pietersburg, SA
C005   lesliei ssp. lesliei var. lesliei (Warrenton form), SA
C036   lesliei ssp. lesliei var. lesliei (Warrenton form), SA
C096   lesliei ssp. lesliei var. lesliei (Warrenton form)/25 km n Kimberley, SA
C005A   lesliei ssp. lesliei var. lesliei acf Albiflora/near Warrenton, SA
C036A   lesliei ssp. lesliei var. lesliei acf Albinica/near Warrenton, SA
C036B   lesliei ssp. lesliei var. lesliei acf Storms´s Albinigold/near Warrenton, SA
C028   lesliei ssp. lesliei var. lesliei/10 km n Harrismith, SA
C031   lesliei ssp. lesliei var. lesliei/10 km ne Meyerton, SA
C342   lesliei ssp. lesliei var. lesliei/10 km ne Pretoria, SA
C007   lesliei ssp. lesliei var. lesliei/15 km s Johannesburg, SA
C331   lesliei ssp. lesliei var. lesliei/15 km sse Pretoria, SA
C010   lesliei ssp. lesliei var. lesliei/25 km sw Lobatse, B (= Botswana)
C358   lesliei ssp. lesliei var. lesliei/25 km w Lobatse, Botswana
C033   lesliei ssp. lesliei var. lesliei/45 km e Pietersburg, SA
C352   lesliei ssp. lesliei var. lesliei/45 km e Pietersburg, SA
C029   lesliei ssp. lesliei var. lesliei/45 km ne Vaalswater, SA
C139   lesliei ssp. lesliei var. lesliei/5 km e Benoni, SA
C115   lesliei ssp. lesliei var. lesliei/5 km nw Vryburg, SA
C026   lesliei ssp. lesliei var. lesliei/60 km sw Johannesburg, SA

C138   lesliei ssp. lesliei var. lesliei/near Benoni, SA
C027   lesliei ssp. lesliei var. lesliei/near Bethlehem, SA
C344   lesliei ssp. lesliei var. lesliei/near Orkney, SA
C018   lesliei ssp. lesliei var. lesliei/near Stella, SA
C343   lesliei ssp. lesliei var. lesliei/near Vanderbylpark, SA
C407   lesliei ssp. lesliei var. lesliei/15 km n Krugersdorp, SA
C141   lesliei ssp. lesliei var. mariae/10 km sw Boshoff, SA
C152   lesliei ssp. lesliei var. mariae/30 km nne Kimberley, SA
C006A   lesliei ssp. lesliei var. minor acf Witblom/25 km sw Swartruggens, SA
C006   lesliei ssp. lesliei var. minor/25 km sw Swartruggens, SA
C204   lesliei ssp. lesliei var. rubrobrunnea/5 km nw Krugersdorp, SA
C017   lesliei ssp. lesliei var. rubrobrunnea/5 km nw Randfontein, SA
C153   lesliei ssp. lesliei var. venteri (maraisii)/60 km nw Kimberley, SA
C001   lesliei ssp. lesliei var. venteri/30 km nw Warrenton, SA (= South-Africa)
C047   lesliei ssp. lesliei var. venteri/30 km w Warrenton, SA

C251   marmorata var. elisae/30 km se Vioolsdrif, SA
C252   marmorata var. elisae/30 km sse Vioolsdrif, SA
C214   marmorata var. elisae/35 km se Vioolsdrif, SA
C260   marmorata var. marmorata (diutina)/15 km ene Steinkopf, SA
C058   marmorata var. marmorata (framesii)/45 km ene Springbok SA
C365   marmorata var. marmorata (framesii)/60 km ne Springbok, SA
C163   marmorata var. marmorata/25 km ne Steinkopf, SA
C360   marmorata var. marmorata/35 km ne Steinkopf, SA
C305   marmorata var. marmorata/40 km nne Steinkopf, SA

C272A   meyeri acf Hammeruby/45 km nne Port Nolloth, SA
C212   meyeri/40 km nne Port Nolloth, SA
C272   meyeri/45 km nne Port Nolloth, SA
C273   meyeri/55 km nne Port Nolloth, SA
C419   meyeri/45 km nne Port Nolloth, SA

C304   naureeniae/60 km se Springbok, SA

C162B   olivacea var. nebrownii/70 km wsw Pofadder, SA
C403   olivacea var. nebrownii/near Aggeneys, SA
C109   olivacea var. olivacea/10 km n Pofadder, SA
C055   olivacea var. olivacea/25 km sw Pofadder, SA

C311   optica (maculate form)/ 45 km se Lüderitz, Namibia
C293   optica (maculate form)/ 95 km sse Lüderitz, Namibia
C291   optica (maculate form)/100 km sse Lüderitz, Namibia
C081A   optica acf Rubra/10 km w Lüderitz, Namibia
C287   optica cv. Rubra/10 km sw Lüderitz, Namibia
C275   optica/10 km n Lüderitz, Namibia
C276   optica/10 km s Lüderitz, Namibia
C277   optica/10 km sw Lüderitz, Namibia
C286   optica/10 km sw Lüderitz, Namibia
C081   optica/10 km w Lüderitz, Namibia
C292   optica/120 km sse Lüderitz, Namibia
C294   optica/140 km sse Lüderitz, Namibia
C310   optica/160 km sse Lüderitz, Namibia
C307   optica/170 km sse Lüderitz, Namibia
C288   optica/40 km sse Lüderitz, Namibia
C289   optica/50 km s Lüderitz, Namibia
C290   optica/65 km s Lüderitz, Namibia
C404   optica/15 km n Bogenfels, Namibia

C414   optica/around Lüderitz Bay, Namibia

C128A   otzeniana acf Aquamarine/35km nnw Loeriesfontein, SA
C128   otzeniana/35 km nnw Loeriesfontein, SA
C350   otzeniana/40 km nnw Loeriesfontein, SA
C280   otzeniana/45 km nnw Loeriesfontein, SA

C264   pseudotruncatella ssp. + var. pseudotrunc. (pallid form)/60 km ssw Windhoek, Namibia
C381   pseudotruncatella ssp. + var. pseudotruncatella (alpina)/ 30 km s Windhoek, Namibia
C068   pseudotruncatella ssp. + var. pseudotruncatella (alpina)/35 km sse Windhoek, Namibia
C100   pseudotruncatella ssp. + var. pseudotruncatella (mundtii)/135 km ne Windhoek, Namibia
C099   pseudotruncatella ssp. + var. pseudotruncatella (mundtii)/150 km ne Windhoek, Namibia
C067   pseudotruncatella ssp. + var. pseudotruncatella/20 km ene Windhoek, Namibia
C070   pseudotruncatella ssp. + var. pseudotruncatella/30 km s Windhoek, Namibia
C104   pseudotruncatella ssp. archerae/120 km nw Maltahöhe, Namibia
C306   pseudotruncatella ssp. archerae/120 km nw Maltahöhe, Namibia
C245   pseudotruncatella ssp. dendritica (farinosa)/55 km ssw Rehoboth, Namibia
C071   pseudotruncatella ssp. dendritica (pulmonuncula)/50 km wnw Rehoboth, Namibia
C384   pseudotruncatella ssp. dendritica/6 km s Rehoboth, Namibia
C072   pseudotruncatella ssp. dendritica/65 km wsw Rehoboth, Namibia
C357   pseudotruncatella ssp. dendritica/75 km sw Rehoboth, Namibia
C073   pseudotruncatella ssp. dendritica/95 km wsw Rehoboth, Namibia
C246   pseudotruncatella ssp. groendrayensis(Witkop form)/55 km s Rehoboth, Namibia
C239   pseudotruncatella ssp. groendrayensis/45 km sse Rehoboth, Namibia
C244   pseudotruncatella ssp. groendrayensis/50 km s Rehoboth, Namibia
C097   pseudotruncatella ssp. pseudotrunc. var. riehmerae (edithiae)/50 km se Windhoek/Namibia
C187   pseudotruncatella ssp. pseudotruncatella var. elisabethiae/55 km ese Otjiwarongo, Namibia
C315   pseudotruncatella ssp. pseudotruncatella var. pseudotruncatella/20 km ene Windhoek, Namibia
C263   pseudotruncatella ssp. pseudotruncatella var. pseudotruncatella/20 km w Windhoek, Namibia
C413   pseudotruncatella ssp. pseudotruncatella var. pseudotruncatella/100 km w Windhoek, Namibia
C069   pseudotruncatella ssp. volkii/45 km s Windhoek, Namibia

C314   ruschiorum var. lineata/40 km ne Cape Fria, Namibia
C386   ruschiorum var. lineata/40 km nne Rocky Point, Namibia
C313   ruschiorum var. lineata/45 km n Rocky Point, Namibia
C380   ruschiorum var. lineata/50 km ene Rocky Point, Namibia
C312   ruschiorum var. lineata/50 km ne Rocky Point, Namibia
C240   ruschiorum var. ruschiorum (nelii)/ 25 km e Cape Cross/Kaap Kruis, Namibia
C102   ruschiorum var. ruschiorum (nelii)/20 km e Cape Cross/Kaap Kruis/Namibia
C316   ruschiorum var. ruschiorum (nelii)/near Cape Cross/Kaap Kruis, Namibia
C387A   ruschiorum var. ruschiorum acf Silver Reed/8 km n Rössing, Namibia
C101   ruschiorum var. ruschiorum/35 km ne Swakopmund, Namibia
C103   ruschiorum var. ruschiorum/45 km ene Henties Bay, Namibia
C241   ruschiorum var. ruschiorum/65 km ene Henties Bay, Namibia
C242   ruschiorum var. ruschiorum/65 km ene Swakopmund, Namibia
C387   ruschiorum var. ruschiorum/8 km n Rössing, Namibia

C086   salicola (maculate form)/35 km se Hopetown, SA
C351A   salicola acf Malachite/10 km w Luckhoff, SA
C034   salicola/10 km nw Luckhoff, SA
C049   salicola/10 km nw Petrusville, SA
C351   salicola/10 km w Luckhoff, SA
C320   salicola/10 km wnw Luckhoff, SA
C353   salicola/15 km wnw Luckhoff, SA
C322   salicola/20 km sw Luckhoff, SA
C321   salicola/25 km wnw Petrusville, SA

C037   salicola/40 km se Hopetown, SA

C184   schwantesii ssp. + var. schwantesii (gulielmi)/10 km nw Helmeringhausen, Namibia
C165   schwantesii ssp. gebseri/70 km s Maltahöhe, Namibia
C248   schwantesii ssp. schwant. var. urikosensis (kunjasensis)/15 km ne Helmeringhausen, Namibia
C186   schwantesii ssp. schwant. var. urikosensis (kunjasensis)/5 km ne Helmeringhausen,Namibia
C144   schwantesii ssp. schwantesii var schwantesii (grey form)/55 km nne Aus, Namibia
C299   schwantesii ssp. schwantesii var. marthae, 120 km sse Aus, Namibia
C148   schwantesii ssp. schwantesii var. marthae/60 km sse Aus, Namibia
C249   schwantesii ssp. schwantesii var. marthae/60 km sse Aus, Namibia
C411   schwantesii ssp. schwantesii var. marthae/75 km se Aus, Namibia
C192   schwantesii ssp. schwantesii var. rugosa/40 km nw Helmeringhausen, Namibia
C247   schwantesii ssp. schwantesii var. rugosa/40 km nw Helmeringhausen, Namibia
C250   schwantesii ssp. schwantesii var. schwantesii (grey form)/120 km se Aus, Namibia
C150   schwantesii ssp. schwantesii var. schwantesii (kuibisensis)/25 km e Aus, Namibia
C211   schwantesii ssp. schwantesii var. schwantesii/10 km se Helmeringhausen, Namibia
C079   schwantesii ssp. schwantesii var. schwantesii/25 km sw Helmeringhausen, Namibia
C164   schwantesii ssp. schwantesii var. schwantesii/25 km sw Helmeringhausen, Namibia
C080   schwantesii ssp. schwantesii var. schwantesii/30 km sw Helmeringhausen, Namibia
C265   schwantesii ssp. schwantesii var. schwantesii/45 km n Helmeringhausen, Namibia
C145   schwantesii ssp. schwantesii var. schwantesii/55 km ne Aus, Namibia
C146   schwantesii ssp. schwantesii var. schwantesii/55 km ne Aus, Namibia
C143B   schwantesii ssp. schwantesii var. schwantesii/60 km nne Aus, Namibia
C191   schwantesii ssp. schwantesii var. schwantesii/60 km nw Helmeringhausen, Namibia
C190   schwantesii ssp. schwantesii var. schwantesii/70 km sw Maltahöhe, Namibia
C076   schwantesii ssp. schwantesii var. schwantesii/70 km w Maltahöhe, Namibia
C106   schwantesii ssp. schwantesii var. schwantesii/80 km w Maltahöhe, Namibia
C077   schwantesii ssp. schwantesii var. schwantesii/near Helmeringhausen, Namibia
C185   schwantesii ssp. schwantesii var. schwantesii/near Helmeringhausen, Namibia
C107   schwantesii ssp. schwantesii var. urikosensis (christinae)/20 km w Maltahöhe, Namibia
C210   schwantesii ssp. schwantesii var. urikosensis (christinae)/45 km w Maltahöhe, Namibia
C074   schwantesii ssp. schwantesii var. urikosensis (christinae)/50 km w Maltahöhe, Namibia
C075   schwantesii ssp. schwantesii var. urikosensis (nutupsdriftensis)/35 km w Maltahöhe, Namibia
C105   schwantesii ssp. schwantesii var. urikosensis/100 km nw Maltahöhe, Namibia
C083   schwantesii ssp. schwantesii var. urikosensis/near Bethanien, Namibia

C388   steineckeana/habitat unknown; hybrid?

C253   terricolor (peersii)/ 95 km nw Port Elizabeth, SA
C254   terricolor (peersii)/30 km ene Willowmore, SA
C376   terricolor (peersii)/35 km ese Willowmore, SA
C131   terricolor (peersii)/near Miller Station, SA
C339   terricolor (peersii)/near Steytlerville, SA
C134   terricolor (Prince Albert form)/5 km n Prince Albert, SA
C345A   terricolor acf Speckled Gold/30 km wnw Prince Albert Road, SA
C132A   terricolor acf Silver Spurs/40 km e Laingsburg, SA
C133   terricolor/25 km s Beaufort West, SA
C130   terricolor/30 km sw Rietbron, SA
C345   terricolor/30 km wnw Prince Albert Road, SA
C346   terricolor/30 km wnw Prince Albert Road, SA
C132   terricolor/40 km e Laingsburg, SA
C379   terricolor/60 km e Prince Albert, SA
C418   terricolor/ne Willowmore, SA

C167   vallis-mariae (margarethae)/near Berseba, Namibia
C282   vallis-mariae/ 125 km n Keetmanshoop, Namibia

C166   vallis-mariae/110 km nne Keetmanshoop, Namibia
C281   vallis-mariae/15 km e Mariental, Namibia
C066   vallis-mariae/20 km e Gibeon Station, Namibia
C060   vallis-mariae/30 km ssw Mariental, Namibia
C296   vallis-mariae/40 km sse Koes; Namibia
C238   vallis-mariae/85 km ne Keetmanshoop, Namibia

C160   verruculosa var. glabra/20 km sse Kenhardt, SA
C177   verruculosa var. glabra/25 km sse Kenhardt, SA
C025   verruculosa var. glabra/30 km e Kenhardt, SA
C157   verruculosa var. verruculosa (inae)/55 km ene Vanwyksvlei, SA
C095   verruculosa var. verruculosa (inae)/55 km sw Prieska, SA
C196   verruculosa var. verruculosa (inae)/85 km s Pofadder, SA
C129   verruculosa var. verruculosa/30 km e Brandvlei, SA
C159   verruculosa var. verruculosa/30 km ene Vanwyksvlei, SA
C120   verruculosa var. verruculosa/30 km n Vanwyksvlei, SA
C230C   verruculosa var. verruculosa/75 km e Gamoep, SA
C200B   verruculosa var. verruculosa/80 km sse Pofadder, SA
C198   verruculosa var. verruculosa/85 km sse Pofadder, SA
C229B   verruculosa var. verruculosa/90 km s Pofadder, SA
C178   verruculosa var. verruculosa/90 km w Kenhardt, SA

C258   villetii ssp. deboeri/35 km ene Gamoep, SA
C230A   villetii ssp. deboeri/75 km e Gamoep, SA
C231   villetii ssp. deboeri/75 km e Gamoep, SA
C197   villetii ssp. kennedyi/75 km s Pofader, SA
C199   villetii ssp. kennedyi/75 km sse Pofadder, SA
C200A   villetii ssp. kennedyi/80 km sse Pofadder, SA
C228   villetii ssp. kennedyi/90 km s Pofadder, SA
C229A   villetii ssp. kennedyi/90 km s Pofadder, SA
C123   villetii ssp. kennedyi/90 km sse Pofadder, SA
C195   villetii ssp. villetii/30 km nne Loeriesfontein, SA
C194   villetii ssp. villetii/60 km nnw Loeriesfontein, SA

C127   viridis/25 km s Loeriesfontein, SA

C188   werneri/25 km nne Usakos, Namibia

Lithops werneri C188

Recommended Literature and Specialised Commercial Sources

- Relevant Literature

Cole, Desmond T. (Monograph, 1988): Lithops - Flowering Stones, Republic of South Africa, Randburg, Acorn Books/Russel Friedman-   Books ISBN 0-6200-9678-0 and ISBN 0-6200-9679-9

New edition in 2005, Cactus & Co. ISBN 88-900511-7-5

Cole, Desmond T   (Monograph, 1987): Madoqua: „Lithops of SWA/Namibia", Department of Agriculture and Nature Conservation, South West Africa

Eggli, Urs   (1994): Sukkulenten (in German), Eugen Ulmer GmbH & Co., Stuttgart, ISBN 3-8001-6512-0

Fearn, Brian   (Monograph, 1981): Lithops, British Cactus and Succulent Society Handbook No. 4, Oxford, UK

Hammer, Steven   (Monograph 1999): Lithops – Treasures of the Veld. British Cactus and Succulent Society, ISBN 0-9020-9964-7, new edition 2010; ISBN 0-9020-9992-2

Heine,Dr. Rudolf   (Monograph, 1986 and 1990, 2nd ed., in German): Lithops - Lebende Steine. Neumann-Verlag, Radebeul, Leipzig, ISBN 3-7402-0095-2

Jainta, Harald   (Monograph, 2017) Wild Lithops, Verlag Klaus Hess, ISBN for Europe 978-3-933117-93-9

Nel, Gert C.   (Monograph, 1964): Lithops. Stellenbosch University, SA

Shimada, Yasuhiko (Monograph in Japanese; many excellent pictures, „The Genus Lithops" 2001, Japan, ISBN 4-8103-4066-X

Smith, Gideon F. et al.	(1998): Mesembs of the World. BRIZA Publications, National Botanical Institute of South Africa, Pretoria, ISBN 1-8750-9313-0
Sprechman, D.L.	(Monograph 1970): Lithops. Associated University Presses, New Jersey, USA
Storms, Ed	(1986): The new growing the Mesembs. Ed Storms, Inc., P.O. Box 775, Azle, TX 76OLO, USA

- Commercial Sources

Beyer, Uwe	Cono's Paradise, Netterhöfe 10, D-56729 Arft 10, Lithops plants by mail-order; www.conos-paradise.com
du Plooy, Frik	P.O. Box 2094, Kocksvlei, 1764 South Africa; Lithops seed and plants by mail-order
Mesa Garden	Plants and seeds of cacti and succulents www.mesagarden.com

Furthermore, there are various shows and exhibitions organised every year by cactus lovers and succulentophiles. Information about such events appears in local newspapers, periodicals, and scientific journals. It is also worth visiting one of the larger garden centres from time to time because the lucky chance of hunting down a stray Lithops beauty cannot be ruled out altogether.

Lithops julii ssp. fulleri var. rouxii

Future Perspectives

It can be presumed that by now nearly all localities of wild-growing Lithops have been discovered in their native territory. And since there seems to be no further potential for plants to be "made by nature", it will finally become necessary to focus on the production of cultivar forms, unless this has not happened already.

The author has chosen the term "production" deliberately because of the obvious trend to eventually "adorn" the plant lobes, on an increasing scale, with spectacular colorations and markings through controlled selection and in-breeding.

And there is many a (commercial) breeder who, letting cultivars "shoot up like mushrooms", will not be guided by economic efficiency alone, but also by the ambition to see his name deeply carved into the annals of Lithops history.

As mentioned earlier on page 30, the cultivar forms are very attractive plants indeed. During the earlier phases of this era, they evolved from natural selection or mutations (occurring both in habitat and in the progeny of cultivated plants), which in itself provides no room for criticism.

Meanwhile, it must be suspected that this cultivar-proliferating begins to, literally, grow into a mania and to set the mark for almost all breeding efforts. Seed lists and the figures below may serve as evidence:

While in 1988 D.T. Cole described 23 cultivars in his book (p. 85), Steven Hammer lists as many as 39 such plants in his work (p. 146), which appeared in 1999. One must take into account that a newly bred cultivar often needs many years and experiments before it becomes stabilised and pure-breeding (and quite a few will never attain 100% true-breeding qualities).

Whereas Nature might have needed millenia, Man has now succeeded in increasing the stock list of these novelties by 70% within 11 years.

If not under way already, genetic engineering will, sooner or later, become the tool for scientists to create the weirdest-looking lobe patterns. Then, perhaps, we shall be afforded the opportunity to admire the star-spangled banner, America's Stars and Stripes, on the leaf tips of a Lithops plant (acf United States?). Myriads of new possibilities would open up, once the genetic information could be decoded and ''at last'' be available for manipulation. On a global scale, the plant and gift industries could probably foresee turnover rates going in the billions!

For those who have interest in Lithops acf "Frankensteinium", please see www.succulent-tissue-culture.com .

At this point - and as warranted in many other instances - one should carefully reconsider whether it is really necessary for Man to recklessly exploit everything within his capabilities.

In the author's view, a responsible nurseryman should always consider it his primary duty to conserve the original genetic material that Nature once made available to us.

Lithops terricolor (C134?)

Happy Conclusion: Acknowledgements

It is appropriate here to thank all those with my heart who helped me accomplish this work. I am also greatly indebted to those who not only provided me with information and advice but also gave me the opportunity to enhance my knowledge and experience about the genus Lithops.

Some of the photographs seen in this book could be taken only with the kind assistance of farmers and guides in Namibia, and of other Lithops enthusiasts who deserve acknowledgement for permitting me to take pictures in their greenhouses.

I am particularly grateful to my wife Rita for her patience and understanding which was always much appreciated, but seldom deserved. For many years now she has been detailed to share my affection with an enormous number of hosted plants, and so she is not always having an easy time of it.

.... chiselled into stone ....

Appendix:

„There is something wrong with them"

(Translated by Vic Knight)

Reasons for the rarity of many Lithops-cultivars

For example, in 1978 Lithops terricolor acf Speckled Gold (C345A) was discovered in habitat, and up to today is comparatively seldom met with in collections. Very lovely plants. Why is this so? Although many enthusiasts are certainly interested in successful future offspring from selective breeding there are fewer plants of these species than desired because nature has put a stop.

Poor Seed Production

In any case, with few available plants there is a reason for it, as capsules of correctly pollinated flowers often remain empty.

Germination Quotas

A further important indicator is to what extent purity in the genetic make-up has been achieved. The germination quota often remains far behind the normal rate. Whilst a quote from 70% up to over 90% with seed of respectable quality is normal, problematic cultivars get stuck with 10% to 35%.

Instability

In addition, complications arise with which, germinated plants are frequently weak and die off. The strong plants are then not seldom the main types from which the cultivar plants once emerged.

Slow Growth

By way of example it is noticeable with Lithops meyeri acf Hammeruby (C272A) that the red plants distinctly lag behind in the growth of their green examples. My own sowing in 2003 shows that the red seedlings between the green ones in the same pot are only about half as large.

Hammeruby requires longer to become adult plants and flower (Steven Hammer reported on this) similarly, this is also known in respect of Lithops salicola acf Bacchus. Some cultivars lag in their size behind the main types.

Flower Indolence

Some species prove to be lazy flowerers like for example Lithops aucampiae acf Betty`s Beryl (C389).

Over Sensitivity

Some cultivar varities with their sensitivity, make the collectors love of something really special additionally difficult. With Lithops julii acf Peppermint Crème (C297A) one should hold back the watering still more than usual.

The last discovered Lithops species, Lithops coleorum (1994) and L. hermetica (1994) have become distibuted in collections in a relatively short time and seed is obtainable at recommended seedsmen at mostly fair prices.

It is admittedly in this connection, not only a matter of cultivars, but also of achetypes it can be proved, on the basis of these examples that with healthy and established inherited material, a quick distribution in collections is possible.

Lithops specialist Klaus Ingenwepelt from Kevelaer, Germany hit the nail on the head with his remark "the rare cultivars are simply lacking something".

The change (mutation) of the outer shape of the plants takes place in some way due to the costs of the genotypes.

Lithops olivacea var. nebrownii acf Red Olive is, according to research by Keith Green (Lithops Scrapbook) 1947(!), mentioned in the Cactus and Succulent Journal of Great Britain. Today it actually still belongs to the rarest of the species.

Lithops salicola acf Bacchus has up to now hardly ever appeared in seed lists.

The aforementioned difficulties apply to several of these species.
There is still a whole range of further cultivated forms which up to now have not become so well known, which deserves the full attention of Lithops enthusiasts.

The stabilisation and distribution of these attractive species is a splendid undertaking, if also a test of patience.

Cultivar List				
species	ssp./var.	acf.	C	Form
amicorum		Freckled Friend	ex 410	sel. pattern
aucampiae	aucampiae	Betty's Beryl	389	G+W-Form
aucampiae	aucampiae	Firebrandt		R-Form
aucampiae	aucampiae	Jackson's Jade	395	G-Form
aucampiae	aucampiae	Storms' Snowcap	392	W-Form
aucampiae	aucampiae	Rubrobrunneus	ex 334?	R-Form
aucampiae	aucampiae	Rudesheim Ruby		R-Form
aucampiae	euniceae	Bellaketty	ex 048	G-Form
aucampiae	euniceae	Hikoruby	ex 048	R-Form
aucampiae	fluminalis	Chieruby	ex 054	R-Form
aucampiae	fluminalis	Green River (Flavivirens)	ex 054	G-Form
bromfieldii	bromfieldii	Noemie's Kiwi	ex 368	G-Form
bromfieldii	bromfieldii	White Nymph (Albiflorus?)	ex 279	W-Form
bromfieldii	glaudinae	Embers	ex 393	R-Form
bromfieldii	insularis	Sulphurea (Ki Meigen)	362	G-Form
dinteri	dinteri	Dintergreen	206A	G-Form
divergens	divergens	Pearl Blush		W-Form
dorotheae		Zorro		sel. pattern
fulviceps	fulviceps	Aurea	363	G+W-Form
gesineae	annae	Hanawared	ex 078	R-Form
gesineae	gesineae	Pink Form	ex 207	R-Form
gracilidelineata		Silwersalm	Hyb	sel. pattern/colour
gracilidelineata	brandbergensis	Vertigo (Greenberg)	ex 394	G-Form
gracilidelineata	Café au Lait X orange brandberg.	Brandcafé	Hyb	Hybrid
gracilidelineata	gracilidelineata	Café au Lait	ex 309	sel. pattern
gracilidelineata	gracilidelineata streyi	Snow Fog	ex 373	sel. pattern
gracilidelineata	gracilidelineata	Ernst's Witkop	385A	W-Form
gracilidelineata	waldroniae	Fritz's White Lady	189A	W-Form
hallii	ochracea	Green Soapstone	111A	G-Form
helmutii		Albiflos		W-Form/hybrid?
hermetica		Green Diamond	397A	G-Form
herrei		Splendido	no numb. rec.	G+W-Form
hookeri	dabneri	Annarosa	ex 301	G+W?-Form
hookeri	dabneri	Choc Top	ex 013	?
hookeri	hookeri	Envy (extict?)	ex 336	G-Form
hookeri	lutea	Aubarede	ex 038	G+W-Form
hookeri	marginata	Shimada's Apricot	ex 053	R-Form
hookeri	susannae	White Susan	ex 091	W-Form
julii	fulleri	Fullergreen	056A	G-Form

julii	fulleri	Limelight	ex 259	G-Form
julii	fulleri	Kikusiyo Giyoku	no numb. rec.	sel. pattern
julii	fulleri	Purple Shell	Hyb	red Hyb.
julii	julii	Peppermint Créme	297A	G-Form
julii	julii	Hot Lips	ex 183	sel. pattern
karasmontana	unknown	Axel's Rose	no numb. rec.	R-Form
karasmontana	aiaisensis	Orange Ice		sel. pattern
karasmontana	eberlanzii	Avocado Cream	370A/402	G-Form
karasmontana	eberlanzii	Purper	ex 369	R-Form
karasmontana	eberlanzii	White Rabbit	Hyb	Hybrid eberl. X ?
karasmontana	karasmontana	Rosary		aberrant growth
karasmontana	karasmontana	Top Red (lateritia)		sel. pattern
karasmontana	lericheana	Red	ex 329	R-Form
karasmontana	lericheana	acf Lerichegreen	ex 329/330?	G-Form
karasmontana	tischeri x lericheana	Lava Flow	Hyb	Hybrid
lesliei	lesliei	Albiflora	ex 005	W-Form
lesliei	lesliei	Albinica	036A	G+W-Form
lesliei	lesliei	Fred's Redhead	ex 005	R-Form
lesliei	lesliei	Inca Gold	036Bx036A	Hybr. Albinigold x Albinica
lesliei	lesliei	Stonesthrow		Hybrid?
lesliei	lesliei	Storms' Albinigold	036B	G-Form
lesliei	hornii	Greenhorn	ex 015	G+W-Form
lesliei	minor	Witblom	006A	W-Form
lesliei	venteri maraisii	Blacktop	ex 153	sel. pattern
lesliei	venteri	Ventergreen	ex 001	G-Form
marmorata	marmorata	Polepský Smaragd	no numb. rec.	G-Form
meyeri		Hammeruby	272A	R-Form
olivacea	nebrownii	Red Olive	ex 162B?	R-Form
olivacea	olivacea	Angels of Tony		aberrant growth
optica		Rubra	081A/287	R-Form
optica		Rubragold		R+Y-Form*
optica		Ruby		fast growing Rubra-Form
otzeniana		Aquamarine	128A	G-Form
otzeniana		Cesky Granat	no numb. rec.	R-Form
pseudotruncatella	archerae	Split Pea	ex 104	G-Form
pseudotruncatella	pseudotruncatella	Albiflora	ex 068	W-Form
pseudotruncatella	riehmerae	Green Ivory	ex 097	G-Form
pseudotruncatella	?	Springbloom		?
ruschiorum	ruschiorum	Silver Reed	387A	W-Form
salicola		Bacchus /Sato's Violet	ex 086?	R-Form
salicola		Daikangyoku	no numb. rec.	sel. pattern
salicola		Malachite	351A	G-Form
schwantesii	rugosa	Blue Moon	ex 247	sel. bluish Form
schwantesii	rugosa	Shagreen	no numb. rec.	G-Form
schwantesii	urikosensis	Nutwerk	ex 075	sel. pattern

schwantesii	urikosensis	Witblom		W-Form
terricolor		Chocolate Sprinkles	ex 134	sel. pattern/colour
terricolor		Green Sandpoort	ex 132?	G-Form
terricolor		Pinky	ex 254?	sel. pinkish Form
terricolor		Silver Spurs	132A	W-Form
terricolor		Speckled Gold	345A	G-Form
terricolor		Steamy Windows	ex 132A	sel. pattern
terricolor		Violetta	ex 132?	R-Form
vallis-mariae		Valley Girl	ex 281	W-Form
verruculosa	verruculosa	Rose of Texas	ex 159	P-Form
verruculosa	verruculosa	Verdigris	ex 159	G-Form

G = green/yellow-gr. form
R = red form
W = white flow. inst. of yellow
Y = yellowflow. inst. of white
P = pink flower
sel. = selected form

www.ingramcontent.com/pod-product-compliance
Lightning Source LLC
Chambersburg PA
CBHW031918270726
48655CB00006BA/2535